"In *Catholicism and Citizenship*, an acco[...]
Vatican II Church situates the novelty of [...]
and the resistance it has provoked—on t[...]
disturbing terrain of global politics and 't[...]
Francis envisions the Church as an engaged member of world society,
missionary and prophetic, yet nonideological and inclusive. To those
dismayed by public vitriol, worried about international politics, or
doubtful that the Church can change the world, this book will bring new
breadth of insight and encouraging seeds of hope."

    —Lisa Sowle Cahill
    Boston College

"Massimo Faggioli is in the first rank of theologians to come of age
since the Second Vatican Council and to study both the Council and
the post-conciliar era. In this book he sets out from *Gaudium et Spes*,
the Council's document on the church in the modern world, to spur
Catholic ecclesiology toward a new engagement with a globalizing world
in political crisis, an engagement in line with Pope Francis's vision of
a missionary church of mercy. *Catholicism and Citizenship* displays
the author's usual skill at analyzing conciliar and later documents
and providing their historical context. He brings to this task a unique
perspective and familiarity not only with Italian but European experience
and theology. Sparks of insight and information fly from every chapter."

    —Peter Steinfels
        Professor Emeritus
        Fordham University
        Former co-director of the Fordham Center on Religion
            and Culture

"With this book, Massimo Faggioli cements his reputation as his
generation's premier interpreter of the relationship between American
Catholics and the Church in Rome. He is incisive, insightful, and
unfailingly constructive in his observations."

    —Cathleen Kaveny
        Libby Professor of Law and Theology
        Boston College

Catholicism and Citizenship

Political Cultures of the Church in the Twenty-First Century

Massimo Faggioli

A Michael Glazier Book

LITURGICAL PRESS

Collegeville, Minnesota

www.litpress.org

A Michael Glazier Book published by Liturgical Press

Cover design by Ann Blattner. Illustrations courtesy of Getty Images.

1   2   3   4   5   6   7   8   9

ISBN 978-0-8146-8423-8   ISBN 978-0-8146-8448-1 (ebook)

To Sarah, Laura, and Gabriel

Contents

"This council exhorts Christians, as citizens of two cities, to strive to discharge their earthly duties conscientiously and in response to the Gospel spirit. They are mistaken who, knowing that we have here no abiding city but seek one which is to come, think that they may therefore shirk their earthly responsibilities. For they are forgetting that by the faith itself they are more obliged than ever to measure up to these duties, each according to their proper vocation."

Second Vatican Council, Pastoral Constitution on the Church in the Modern World, *Gaudium et Spes*, December 7, 1965, par. 43

Abbreviations

SC *Sacrosanctum Concilium*, Constitution on the Sacred
Liturgy, 1963

IM *Inter Mirifica*, Decree on the Means of Social
Communication, 1963

LG *Lumen Gentium*, Dogmatic Constitution on the Church,
1964

OE *Orientalium Ecclesiarum*, Decree on the Catholic Churches
of the Eastern Rite, 1964

UR *Unitatis Redintegratio*, Decree on Ecumenism, 1964

CD *Christus Dominus*, Decree on the Pastoral Office of Bishops
in the Church, 1965

PC *Perfectae Caritatis*, Decree on the Adaptation and Renewal
of Religious Life, 1965

OT *Optatam Totius*, Decree on Priestly Formation, 1965

GE *Gravissimum Educationis*, Declaration on Christian
Education, 1965

NA *Nostra Aetate*, Declaration on the Relation of the Church to
Non-Christian Religions, 1965

DV *Dei Verbum*, Dogmatic Constitution on Divine Revelation,
1965

AA *Apostolicam Actuositatem*, Decree on the Apostolate of the
Laity, 1965

DH *Dignitatis Humanae*, Declaration on Religious Freedom,
1965

AG *Ad Gentes*, Decree on the Mission Activity of the Church,
1965

PO   *Presbyterorum Ordinis*, Decree on the Ministry and Life of
      Priests, 1965

GS   *Gaudium et Spes*, Pastoral Constitution on the Church in the
      Modern World, 1965

Given the differences in the quality of the translations into English
of the conciliar documents, the quotations of conciliar documents
are taken in some cases from the Vatican website; in other cases from
Vatican Council II: Constitutions, Decrees, Declarations, edited by
Austin Flannery (Northport, NY: Costello, 1996); and in other cases
from *The Documents of Vatican II*, edited by Walter M. Abbott, SJ,
and translation editor Joseph Gallagher (New York: Guild Press,
1966). I have sometimes made some minor changes.

Acknowledgments

This book is the result of two decades of research on Vatican II. But it was not a coincidence that these pages were written and the project was conceived during a particular moment in the life of American politics, that is, during the campaign for the presidential election of November 2016. The election of Donald Trump indeed poses many questions to the Catholic Church about its recent political stances and its position in the future of the United States and in the world.

But the question of the social and political message and position of the Catholic Church in the modern world will continue to remain central even after the end of a political season marked by, among other things, a deep polarization within the Catholic Church and a crisis in the theological ethos of the public engagement of Catholics in the public square, particularly in the western world, which Roman Catholicism once used to identify as its historical and cultural cradle.

The crisis of that engagement is deeper and graver than the mere crisis of political Catholicism in terms of the political engagement of Catholics with or without a Catholic party. It is a crisis related to an interpretation of the trajectories of modernity, which in turn is closely connected to a historical and theological hermeneutic of the Second Vatican Council. The lectures delivered during the years 2015 and 2016 offered me the opportunity to link my research on Vatican II to a particular historical and theological Catholic moment in the United States. These pages represent an attempt to make clear what is at stake when the Catholic Church overlooks or misinterprets the conciliar ecclesiology of the church in the modern world—or better, in the original Latin, "in the world of this time"—the title of the constitution *Gaudium et Spes: De ecclesia in mundo huius temporis*.

This book is also a result of my experience as a European Catholic historian and theologian who came to the United States in 2008. In this sense, this book is one further step in my dealing in a deeper and more direct way with global Catholicism from the particular angle of the Catholic Church in the United States. This is true for this book more than for my previous books, and it is a way of continuing my analysis of the pontificate of Pope Francis and in particular the reception of Francis by the Catholic Church in the United States.

I thank here the University of St. Thomas (St. Paul, Minnesota) for making possible the sabbatical semester granted during the spring semester 2016. Among my colleagues at the University of St. Thomas, I am grateful to those who were on the board of the Institute for Catholicism and Citizenship during the academic year 2015–2016, and in particular to Michael Hollerich and Gerald Schlabach for the continuing conversation on these matters. John O'Malley, SJ, continues to be my first partner in dialogue: his book *What Happened at Vatican II* (2008) opened a new season of reflections on the council, whose significance is now particularly clear in light of the pontificate of Pope Francis. Mark Massa, SJ, is a constant source of inspiration and much needed laughter, and he was the one who introduced me, in his graduate course as the Gasson Chair at Boston College in the spring semester of 2009, to the intricate issue of the relationship between America and Catholicism. Peter Hünermann, many years ago, held a seminar in Tübingen on Catholic ecclesiology in the twentieth century that was decisive in forming my approach to the Catholic tradition: most of all, he is for me an example of the way a citizen, a theologian, and a Catholic should engage the church, the academy, and the public square. I cannot forget here those with whom I have shared part of these reflections: Steven Millies in the United States; Marcello Neri, Serena Noceti, and Antonio Spadaro, SJ, in Italy; Ormond Rush and Michael Kelly, SJ, in Australia; Sandra Arenas and Carlos Schickendantz in Chile.

This book also builds a bridge between my seven years at the University of St. Thomas (2009–2016) and the beginning of my tenure at Villanova University in the fall semester of 2016. These reflections do not address directly Augustine's legacy and the reception of his thought in terms of the theology of the relationship between the church and the *polis*, and they express the intention of a renewed, close encounter with the Augustinian tradition.

My research on the ecclesiology and the reception of the Second Vatican Council culminated in a series of lectures delivered between 2015 and 2016. In the broad network of people who created the occasions and opportunities for this research to become a book I want to thank here those who invited me to share these reflections in the form of lectures: the Association of US Catholic Priests, the Conference of Major Superiors of Men, the Cathedral Ministry Conference, St. Mary's University (San Antonio, Texas), St. Norbert College (De Pere, Wisconsin), the Pontifical Catholic University of Chile and the Alberto Hurtado University (Santiago, Chile), the Loyola Institute at Trinity College Dublin, and the National Council of Priests of Australia. This book is also the result of my undergraduate and graduate courses on the Second Vatican Council, on ecclesiology, and on Catholicism and political modernity: the input coming from my students continues to be an integral part of my research.

Liturgical Press and in particular Hans Christoffersen have been very encouraging and welcomed this project from the beginning. It is always a great pleasure to work with Lauren L. Murphy, managing editor at Liturgical Press. The intellectual community formed by *Commonweal* has been a constant point of reference even before my arrival in the United States of America, and these reflections owe a great debt to that community of editors, authors, and readers. Robert Mickens at *La Croix International* helped me grow in my attempt to bridge theology and analysis of all things Catholic. My Italian friends and colleagues at the magazines *Il Regno*, *Jesus*, and *Il Mulino* encouraged me to reflect on my American experience in a way that I did not imagine possible when I arrived in the summer of 2008.

This book is dedicated to the many colleagues and friends that I have met thanks to the visible and invisible network that is the Catholic Church, a world in itself.

Villanova University
November 20, 2016
Feast of Christ the King

>⊱

Two of the chapters of this book have appeared elsewhere and have been revised and updated for the present book. I wholeheartedly thank the editors and publishers of the journals and books in which they originally appeared.

The chapter "Inter-Ecclesial Relations and the Public Square: Bishops vs. Religious Orders Between Vatican II and the Post–Vatican II Era" was originally published as "The Ecclesiology of Vatican II as a New Framework for Consecrated Life," in *Origins*, September 10, 2015, Volume 45, Number 15, pp. 255–62.

The chapter "Church and World in Pope Francis's Ecclesiological Shift: Evolution or Crisis of the New Ecclesial Movements?" was originally published in German as "Die Ekklesiologie von Papst Franziskus und die neuen katholischen Bewegungen: Evolution oder Krise?" in *Una Sancta* 71, no. 1 (2016): 18–29.

Introduction

Periodization is an important way for historians and theologians to understand the Catholic Church, and it is also important for the Catholic Church to understand itself. Periodization divides church history into periods marked by some kind of coherence, periods opened and closed by epoch-changing events. Periodization helps us structure history so that we can better understand what is distinctive of a particular period of time in the life of the church. From this point of view, there is no doubt that Catholicism today lives in the post–Vatican II period that started already during Vatican II. But the expression "post-conciliar period" is still a rather vague way to identify the last five decades of Catholicism. The unstable narratives of what the Catholic Church has become after Vatican II require, in this case, an undeniable elusiveness in the label.

The problem is that we know fairly well what happened at Vatican II, but we do not really know what happened during post–Vatican II Catholicism in the global church. Local experiences and narratives vary in a significant way; the points of view of historians, theologians, and pastors often diverge. Nevertheless, we know that within the first fifty years of this post–Vatican II period the global Catholic Church has gone through two major epoch-changing ruptures: the post-9/11 religiously inspired terrorist violence, and the sexual abuse scandal in the Catholic Church.

For those who have paid attention to the effects of these events, it is clear that they question radically and publicly two key assumptions for a Catholic mind-set marked by the mantra of unchangeability: the idea of a perfect continuity in church history and the idea of the possibility of a church almost isolated and unperturbed by what happens outside, *extra ecclesiam*.

September 11, 2001, has redefined the pattern of relationship between the state, civil society, and religions that we have inherited from the early modern period and that lasted until the end of the twentieth century. September 11, 2001, has redrawn the space of theologies, including Catholic theology, not only in the academic context but also in the public sphere of living together. A theology that looks only to its own religious community has become an unusable artifact. The post-9/11 era of global terrorism has redefined the boundaries between church and state: the church is better equipped than the secular state for the delicate operation of symbolic resignification of these invisible but crucial boundaries—boundaries between church and state, between religion and politics, between faith and unbelief, and between different religions among themselves. This is one of the reasons that make world public opinion call the Catholic Church and especially the papacy to speak on the relations between Islam and terrorism, often hoping to obtain from the pope a theological condemnation of the political enemies of the secular state in the western world. This means that the nature of ecclesiology has changed in the post-9/11 world, in a way that may recall the seventeenth century and the end of the wars of religion in Europe. But the path of the ecclesiological self-understanding of Catholicism is still on the trajectory initiated by Vatican II more than fifty years ago.

On the other hand, the sexual abuse scandal had a chastening and humiliating effect on the self-awareness of the Catholic Church: in order to purify itself and start a process of reparation (which is right and just) and reconciliation (as much as possible in a preferential option for the victims), the church needed and still needs the power of the secular state to find the truth. Historically, this is one of the many examples in history in which Catholicism has been pushed from the outside to reform itself. Theologically, the sex abuse scandal is more evidence of the dangers of an ecclesiology of perfect society, the *societas perfecta*—both in its pre–Vatican II version and in its postmodern versions—but it is especially evidence of the end of that religious ideology typical of Christendom.

It is therefore clear to me that the beginning of the twenty-first century has provided the church with abundant evidence of the necessity of reexamining the relationship between the church and the modern world. This book tries to proceed on this path with a focus on the meaning, legacy, and reception in the world of today of Vatican II's Pastoral Constitution on the Church in the Modern World, *Gaudium et Spes*. In these chapters I make an argument in favor of the rediscovery of paragraph 43 of *Gaudium et Spes*, which amounts to an anti-sectarian statement in Catholicism today. This book is a call for a new engagement with the ecclesiology of Vatican II that went beyond the classical, pre–Vatican II division of work between clergy (dealing with the sacred) and the laity (reconquering the secular).

The focus on *Gaudium et Spes* is not only based on the importance of the constitution itself, the last document of the council, a recapitulation of the accomplishments of the council in terms of theological method, but also on the assumption that this particular moment in the life of the church, beginning with the pontificate of Pope Francis on March 13, 2013, cannot be understood without a new appraisal of this document. The pastoral constitution has aged considerably since Vatican II and needs a historically informed hermeneutic. At the same time, *Gaudium et Spes* is a key document in the conciliar identity of this church as well as a key to understanding Pope Francis, exactly because Francis sees in *Gaudium et Spes* not a list of formulations but the manifesto of a new theological method and a new ecclesiological orientation.

This book tries to reframe the ecclesiology of Vatican II for a world "of this time" that has changed enormously since the 1960s. At the same time, it is a world Catholicism that cannot be understood theologically without the ecclesiological reorientation of the council and its culmination in *Gaudium et Spes*. Francis's use of *Gaudium et Spes* (for example, in his teachings, in his intention of calling the Bishops' Synods of 2014–2015, and in his exchanges with the Synods' conclusions) is directly connected to the way the Catholic Church, and Francis in it, reads "the signs of the times": in particular, the shift in the dialogue between church and world from modernity to postmodernity, and with it the emergence of neo-sectarian temptations and neo-integralist and neo-traditionalist nostalgia within western Christianity, including Roman Catholicism. Francis is also a response of the global Catholic Church to these re-actions. Much of the resistance against Francis within Catholicism is rooted in the nostalgia for anti-modernist church teaching and was unleashed by the challenge that Francis brought to the ideologues of a self-sufficient ideological and cultural Catholicism.

A particular focus of this book is the issue of the political culture of Vatican II and its contribution to our public debate about the future of freedom and democracy. I move from the assumption that it is impossible to understand the crisis of democracy in the western world today without a theological framework: modern Catholicism and political modernity have a very complicated relationship that historical-theological literature will need to address soon again. This has become more complicated recently, because of the disconnect between theological discourse and political and cultural elites, and because of the unlearning of the vocabulary of political Catholicism by Catholics themselves—phenomena that are related to the extinction of the old elites of political Catholicism, but that must be explained also with what happened within the ecclesial and ecclesiastical sphere.

This book represents an attempt to contribute from a Catholic perspective to the debate on the role of the church in pluralistic democracy. It is a call for a renewed theological and ecclesial engage-ment with our political realm during a moment of deep crisis that undermines worldwide the legitimacy of democracy. Thus far the desacralization of politics did not mean taking distance from the idol-atry of ideologies and of identities. Rather, desacralization of politics today translates into the loss of the sense of a mutual commitment to others. The radical secularization of our trust in politics as a com-mitment to the duty of becoming neighbors is something that should invite the Catholic Church to reflect more deeply about the relations between Christian faith and *polis*. In the still fairly recent history of the twentieth century, democratic systems respectful of human rights developed in many nation states around the world: it was part of the "joys and hopes" of Vatican II. But today the nation state is incapable of dealing with globalization, and the crisis of democracy is part of this heterogenesis of the democratic idea.

Confronted with this crisis, this book makes no big claims. Rather, it is an exercise in rediscovering what has been forgotten or dismissed about the political cultures and social imagination of the Second Vatican Council. The case for a public Catholicism needs to go back to Vatican II, which defined the church "as sacrament—a sign and instrument of communion with God and of the unity of the entire human race" (GS 42). The emphasis in this book is on the constitution *Gaudium et Spes*, but not without renewed attention to the whole corpus of Vatican II, including the Declaration on Religious Liberty (*Dignitatis Humanae*) (especially in light of the US bishops' campaign on the subject during the latest decade) and the Decree on the Adaptation and Renewal of Religious Life (*Perfectae Caritatis*). This book can also be read as another step in my research on the ecclesiology of Vatican II and its significance in the public square, which started with other two books published by Liturgical Press, *True Reform: Liturgy and Ecclesiology in* Sacrosanctum Concilium (2012), and *Sorting Out Catholicism: A Brief History of the New Ecclesial Movements* (2014).

These reflections open with an analysis of the deep political motivations for the balance of power, defined by Vatican II, between the papacy and the bishops on one side and the clergy and religious orders on the other side, and what that new balance of power meant for the prophetic voice of the Catholic Church. The second chapter addresses the issue of the role of the new Catholic movements *ad extra* during the pontificate of Pope Francis, who has changed significantly the emphasis of the papal magisterium about this Catholic vanguard in secular and pluralistic society. The third chapter challenges one of the paradigms for the church facing pluralism—hegemony or persecution—with particular attention to the church in the United States. In a similar way, chapters 4, 5, and 6 develop a few reflections around issues that are typical of American Christianity and of American Catholicism: the complex legacy of the Constantinian age, the theological issue of the modern world in American Catholicism, and the problem of polarization in a church that Pope Francis described as a polyhedron in the foundational document of his pontificate, the Apostolic Exhortation *Evangelii Gaudium*.

Francis has reopened the ecclesiological debate on the Christian character of the Roman Catholic Church, but he has also offered a view of politics, state, and government that comes from Vatican II and from his lived experience of the council in that key part of the contemporary global Catholic Church that is Latin America. This book wants to be a contribution to an analysis of the political cultures of the Catholic Church as they were expressed at the Second Vatican Council more than fifty years ago, and as they continue to be part of the deep theological and ecclesiological consciousness of the Catholic Church worldwide.

Chapter One

Inter-Ecclesial Relations and the Public Square

Bishops versus Religious Orders between Vatican II and the Post–Vatican II Era

Introduction

The discourse on Catholicism in the world of today is not just influenced by our perception of *what* happened to the church and the world in these last fifty years after Vatican II. It is also driven by a perception of *who* led the church in these last fifty years. In this sense, our perception is correctly focused on the episcopate, which at Vatican II and in the post–Vatican II church has retained and strengthened its role of leadership.

But in order to capture correctly what happened to the power within the Catholic Church in these last fifty years, it is necessary to take a look at other church actors, in particular at those ecclesial actors whose ecclesial-political trajectory after Vatican II has been very different from the trajectory of the bishops. The most interesting case is that of the religious orders, also because—this is especially true of women's religious orders—they recently became the subject of investigations by the Vatican and the bishops in the United States.[1] The current instances of opposition between the episcopate and the religious orders are part of the long history of

---

[1] I am referring here to the six-year-long investigation of the Leadership Conference of Women Religious (LCWR), the main umbrella group for the leaders of women's religious orders in the United States.

the church, which in some cases changed the course of the history of such key institutions as the universities, when Thomas Aquinas in Paris changed the idea of a university by defending, against the opposition of the secular (diocesan) clergy, the right of members of religious orders to become teaching faculty.[2]

But the tensions of these last few years are revelatory of deep tensions within the church between different kinds of actors. These tensions, along with his interpretation of Vatican II, came to a shift with the election of Pope Francis.

1. Francis, the Religious Orders, and the Interpretation of Vatican II

The pontificate of Pope Francis has introduced a paradigm shift in the way the papacy interprets Vatican II both as a corpus of documents and as an event. It is not simply a more "liberal" or "progressive" interpretation of it; instead it is seeing Vatican II as a pivotal event in church history that cannot be overshadowed by the issues surrounding the interpretation of the post–Vatican II period.

Pope Francis, who was ordained a priest in 1969, after the conclusion of the council, moves the church forward with respect to the memory of the council and, for this reason, must manage a legacy that is not that simple: during the pontificate of Benedict XVI, the subject of "Vatican II" was again the cause of controversy so that it came to characterize the Vatican's doctrinal policy in the Ratzinger period, beyond the intentions of Pope Benedict XVI. The way in which Pope Francis "speaks" of the council with his episcopal style is also indicative of his approach to the entire previous pontificate and of the magisterial legacy of Pope Benedict XVI. Pope Francis sees in the Second Vatican Council one of the conditions of the existence of the contemporary church, without the need for the pope himself to go into fine hermeneutic distinctions to apply the council's teach-

---

[2] See Pasquale Porro, *Thomas Aquinas: A Historical and Philosophical Profile*, trans. Joseph Trabbick and Roger W. Nutt (Washington, DC: The Catholic University of America Press, 2016).

ings.[3] In this sense, Francis, the first post-conciliar pope, has in a way liberated Vatican II from the period of controversies—something that only someone not personally involved in Vatican II itself, fifty years ago, could do.

The key role of Vatican II for the pontificate is very clear in Pope Francis's most important acts and documents, from the apostolic exhortation *Evangelii Gaudium* (November 24, 2013) to the encyclical *Laudato Sì* (May 24, 2015), and including the Bull of Indiction of the Extraordinary Jubilee of Mercy (*Misericordiae Vultus*, April 11, 2015). Despite the narrative of Vatican II as the beginning of the decline for religious orders, Francis has maintained his interpretation of Vatican II also in his addresses to the religious. In Pope Francis's Apostolic Letter to All Consecrated People on November 21, 2014, he acknowledges Vatican II as the beginning of a "fruitful path of renewal that, with its lights and shadows, has been a time of grace marked by the presence of the Holy Spirit."[4]

This rediscovery of Vatican II is not limited only to the words and acts of the pope; it has also affected the way the Vatican deals with the religious—and here I am not referring only to the tensions with the LCWR. Francis's interpretation of Vatican II is part of this new climate. The second Letter to All Consecrated People (*Scrutate*, September 23, 2014), published by the Congregation for Institutes of Consecrated Life and Societies of Apostolic Life, issues an invitation "to re-examine the steps taken in the last fifty years. In this memory Vatican II emerges as an event of extreme importance for the renewal of consecrated life."[5]

---

[3] See Massimo Faggioli, *Pope Francis: Tradition in Transition* (New York and Mahwah, NJ: Paulist Press, 2015); Massimo Faggioli, *A Council for the Global Church: Receiving Vatican II in History* (Minneapolis: Fortress Press, 2015).

[4] Pope Francis, Letter to All Consecrated People on the Occasion of the Year of Consecrated Life, November 27, 2014, https://w2.vatican.va/content /francesco/en/apost_letters/documents/papa-francesco_lettera-ap_20141121 _lettera-consacrati.html.

[5] See Congregazione per gli Istituti di Vita Consacrata e le Società di Vita Apostolica, *Scrutate. Ai consacrati e alle consacrate in cammino sui segni di Dio* (Città del Vaticano: Libreria Editrice Vaticana, 2014).

In this particular time in the history of the pontificate and of the reception of Vatican II fifty years after its conclusion, and in light of the recent developments in the role of the religious orders in the Catholic Church, it is the task of a church historian and historian of Vatican II to say something: (1) on the history of Vatican II's Decree on the Adaptation and Renewal of Religious Life (*Perfectae Caritatis*) in the wider perspective of the entire council; (2) on contextualizing the document and its reception in light of the magisterial reception of Vatican II; (3) on the attempts to formulate a few hypotheses about the particular role of the renewal of consecrated life not just in the history of the reception in the past but as a work still to be done.

In order to do this, I will proceed, first, with a section on ecclesiology and religious orders at Vatican II; second, with a section on the reception of the decree *Perfectae Caritatis* and the ecclesiology of Vatican II; third, with a section on the relationship between ecclesiology and socio-political change and its consequences for religious life; and finally, with a section on the good use of the ecclesiology of Vatican II for religious orders and for Catholicism in the public square.

2. Ecclesiology and Religious Orders at Vatican II

In an analysis of the debate on the renewal of religious life at Vatican II, the first interesting fact to emerge is that anxieties about the future of the religious orders were already present in the mid-twentieth century: "concerns about declining number of vocations, aging and overworked religious, ministerial burnout, and loss of an authentic religious spiritual life were major issues for the church hierarchy in the first half of the twentieth century; they were not simply a post–Vatican II phenomenon."[6]

Between the pre–Vatican II years and the years in which the council was in session, the issue of religious orders was mostly "institutional," that is, it concerned their relationship with Rome and

---

[6] Maryanne Confoy, "Religious Life in the Vatican II Era: 'State of Perfection' or Living Charism?," in *50 Years On: Probing the Riches of Vatican II*, ed. David G. Schultenover (Collegeville, MN: Liturgical Press, 2015), 393.

with their members (whether the governance of the orders should be centralized or whether there should be federations of religious orders) and their relationship with the episcopate and the local bishops (the issues of the exemption).[7] In this sense the debate at Vatican II is more about the *place* of religious orders and much less about their *role*, and that is why the debate on the religious at Vatican II is more a continuation of arguments that were already taking place before the council than about something belonging to the council proper.

2.1. Other Documents of Vatican II and the Religious

The problem was not just with what eventually became the decree *Perfectae Caritatis*, but with the theology of religious orders at Vatican II. "A majority of the bishops were opposed to including a special section on religious life because there was a belief first that religious life was not a fundamental structure of the church but rather a beautiful decoration that had developed over the course of the centuries. They thought that while it beautified the church, it wasn't essential to the church. You could dispense with it and the church would still stand."[8]

The ecclesiology of Vatican II is not only in the ecclesiological constitution and in *Gaudium et Spes*, but in all the documents. Vatican II is an act before it is a corpus of documents. Therefore, the ecclesiology of Vatican II as it concerns the religious life is visible already in the act of the council, in the way it unfolded. A paradoxical fact is that the most important theologians and periti at the council were members of religious orders, especially Dominicans and Jesuits,

---

[7] I want to thank here Alessandro Cortesi for sharing with me the draft of his commentary on the decree *Perfectae Caritatis* for the forthcoming volume in the new commentary on the documents of Vatican II published in Italian by Edizioni Dehoniane Bologna and edited by Serena Noceti and Roberto Repole (9 vols., 2014–2018). See also Joachim Schmiedl, *Das Konzil und die Orden: Krise und Erneuerung des gottgeweihten Lebens* (Vallendar-Schönstatt: Patris, 1999).

[8] Joseph W. Tobin, "How Did We Get Here? The Renewal of Religious Life in the Church since Vatican II," in *A Future Built on Faith: Religious Life and the Legacy of Vatican II*, ed. Gemma Simmonds (Dublin: Columba, 2014), 20.

but they never managed to bring to the table the issue of the role of the religious orders; further, in the years before Vatican II these theologians had been marginalized within their own communities in the aftermath of the sanctions issued by the Holy Office against them. The very weak presence of the religious orders at the council is even more significant for the final text of *Perfectae Caritatis* because of the division between the majority and the minority at the council. Particularly absent is the idea that "essential to religious life is the commitment to a *community* as a way of intensifying obedience to the Gospel."[9] Institutionally the ecclesiology of Vatican II deals with religious orders as an element that does not quite fit the transition from a universalist church to a church made up of local churches, from a sociological and juridical ecclesiological vocabulary to a communional and sacramental one, and from an exclusivist to an inclusivist and ecumenical idea of the church.

The ecclesiological shift in the documents of Vatican II begins with the debate on the liturgy. In my book *True Reform*, I made a case for the ecclesiological role of the Constitution on the Sacred Liturgy (*Sacrosanctum Concilium*), the first document debated and approved by the council.[10] In this constitution there is a strong christological and ecumenical recentering of the liturgy, but also present is the idea that there is in a sense "one" liturgy in which the diversity of Catholicity emerges: it is a model that assumes the limitation to monastic communities of certain liturgical practices such as the liturgy of the hours. (An attempt within the liturgical commission to "monasticize" the liturgical reform was defeated.)[11]

---

[9] Gregory Baum, "Commentary," in *The Decree on the Renewal of Religious Life of Vatican Council II*, trans. Austin Flannery (New York: Paulist Press, 1966), 41.

[10] See Massimo Faggioli, *True Reform: Liturgy and Ecclesiology in* Sacrosanctum Concilium (Collegeville, MN: Liturgical Press, 2012).

[11] See Massimo Faggioli, "The Pre-Conciliar Liturgical Movement in the United States and the Liturgical Reform of Vatican II," in *La théologie catholique entre intransigeance et renouveau. La réception des mouvements préconciliaires à Vatican II*, ed. Philippe J. Roy, Gilles Routhier, and Karim Schelkens (Leuven: Brepols, 2011), 69–89.

The most direct document on ecclesiology is the Constitution on the Church (*Lumen Gentium*), whose ecclesiology manifests the shift from the *societas perfecta* to a church as a communion and a people of God, from a mostly juridical vocabulary to a biblical and spiritual description. But *Lumen Gentium* also elevates the episcopate to the highest level, thus making the bishop the point of reference or the standard for the idea of ordained ministry, and it articulates the concept of the priesthood of all believers and the universal call to holiness without specifically defining the religious and consecrated.[12] This is especially important if we connect *Lumen Gentium* to the Decree on the Apostolate of the Laity (*Apostolicam Actuositatem*) and its key message of lay apostolate as genuine participation, together with the hierarchy, in the mission of the church.

The Constitution on the Church in the Modern World (*Gaudium et Spes*) touches on the role of the religious in the church in multiple ways, especially two. First, it redefines the relationship between the church and the world in a way that disavows the *fuga mundi* as an option if based on the idea of a necessary separateness between church and world. This challenges the religious to reconsider the language used to describe the lifestyle of certain communities and their traditions. Second, it brings back into Catholic theology the criterion of historicity—beginning with the "signs of the times" of GS 4—as a necessary element of the consciousness of modernity, and this constitutes a challenge for religious orders and spiritual traditions called to renew themselves in restoring the legacy of the founders, many of whom were chronologically situated in a period in the history of ecclesiology that Vatican II was leaving behind, especially the medieval and Counter Reformation periods.

The Decree on the Ministry and Life of Priests (*Presbyterorum Ordinis*) assumed a few ideas about the ministry: the parish is normative for ministry, the community is composed of the faithful (with obvious problems when we connect ministry and evangelization), and the minister is in hierarchical communion with his bishop. The same

---

[12] Chapter 6 (paragraphs 43–47) of *Lumen Gentium* reveals a striking distance between that text and the reality of religious life.

assumptions are operative in the Decree on the Pastoral Ministry of Bishops (*Christus Dominus*). Quoting John O'Malley, we can say that "for all their merit *Christus Dominus, Presbyterorum Ordinis*, and *Optatam Totius* do not take into sufficient account the tradition of ministry and priesthood in the religious orders."[13] In particular, the understanding of ministry found in *Presbyterorum Ordinis* is difficult to reconcile with the *ad extra* dimension of the church of Vatican II as described in the Decree on Ecumenism (*Unitatis Redintegratio*), in the Declaration on the Relation of the Church with Non-Christian Religions (*Nostra Aetate*), and in the views on atheism found in *Lumen Gentium* and *Gaudium et Spes*.

The ecclesiology of Vatican II opens a new path for the role of the religious in the church, but mostly in an indirect way—for the *spaces* opened by the council are for the church in general without a specific *role* for the religious. In this sense there is a precise historical-theological turn in the ecclesiology of Vatican II that is difficult to reconcile with the role of the religious. *First*, the ecclesiology of Vatican II comes from a *patristic model centered on the bishop, the local church, and its presbyterium*, with a substantial dismissal of other models of Christian community. *Second*, the other pole, the "universal church," is identified much more with *the papacy and the college of bishops* around him than with other expressions of Catholic "globalism," such as the religious orders. *Third*, the ecclesiology of Vatican II considers the patristic model and *the first millennium as much more normative than the second millennium* and especially sees itself as a new age after the end of the Counter Reformation period (including the "long nineteenth century" of which John O'Malley writes in his *What Happened at Vatican II*)[14]— which is exactly the period of expansion of the religious orders.[15]

---

[13] For this section, see John W. O'Malley, "Priesthood, Ministry, and Religious Life: Some Historical and Historiographical Considerations," *Theological Studies* 49 (1988): 223–57, at 253.

[14] See John W. O'Malley, *What Happened at Vatican II* (Cambridge, MA: Belknap Press, 2008).

[15] See Neil Ormerod, *Re-Visioning the Church: An Experiment in Systematic-Historical Ecclesiology* (Minneapolis: Fortress Press, 2014), 329–31. See also

2.2. *Perfectae Caritatis* between Return to the Origins and *Aggiornamento*

Now if we look at the Decree on the Adaptation and Renewal of Religious Life, the picture becomes more interesting in light of the history of the decree. It is not a mystery that the history of *Perfectae Caritatis* is one of the most complicated in the whole history of the documents of Vatican II. Here we see one of the "dark sides" of the very important—indeed, pivotal—focus of Vatican II on the episcopate and episcopal collegiality: not only the clergy but also the religious orders were overlooked in the council's ecclesiological debate of Vatican II. The complicated history of *Perfectae Caritatis* is a good example of how the bishops at Vatican II dealt with an issue that was uncomfortable for most of them.

The schema on the religious started as a juridical-canonical text that avoided theological issues, which were reserved to the doctrinal commission steered by the Holy Office. Since the preparation period (1960–1962) and for a good part of the debate at the council, the attention was almost exclusively focused on the issue of the exemption of the religious orders from the jurisdiction of the local bishops in their dioceses: the bishops at Vatican II had a problem with both the Roman Curia and the religious orders because they were both limiting their monarchical power.

It became clear, as the council unfolded, that if it was true that a council was addressing the reform of religious orders for the first time after Trent (session XXV, *Decretum de Regularibus et Monialibus*), it was also true that the criterion of the *aggiornamento* was simply an invitation to the religious to restore the legacy of the founders in tension with a general renewal or reform of the church.[16] (Noteworthy here is the absence of women in the commission compared with the

---

Severino Dianich, "L'episcopato, ovvero la figura dell'uno. Rilettura teologica," in *Da Montini a Martini: il Vaticano II a Milano*, vol. 1: *Le figure*, ed. Gilles Routhier, Luca Bressan, and Luciano Vaccaro (Brescia: Morcelliana, 2012), 221–41.

[16] See Joseph A. Komonchak, "The Struggle for the Council during the Preparation of Vatican II (1960–1962)," in *History of Vatican II*, ed. Giuseppe Alberigo, English version ed. Joseph A. Komonchak, vol. 1 (New York: Orbis Books, 1995), esp. 185–87.

importance of women religious in the church). The tensions between these two poles—the return to the origins and *aggiornamento* in a church in a new relationship with the modern world—was also evident during the debate on chapter 4 of *De Ecclesia*, which became chapter 6 of *Lumen Gentium*. The marginalization of the debate on the religious during the second session in 1963 put the issue "in a limbo" that was revealing of the council's lack of preparation to debate it.[17] The idea of *accommodata renovatio* (return to the origins and *aggiornamento* for the modern world) became the guiding principle given by the coordinating commission of the council to the commission *de religiosis* on November 29, 1963—but under the threat that many juridical aspects of the reform would be postponed to the reform of the Code of Canon Law. The commission decided on the title *De Accommodata Renovatio Vitae Religiosae* in October 1964, which was also the title of the Roman Curia Congregation's decree *De Religiosis* of March 26, 1956.[18] (But interestingly enough, *Perfectae Caritatis* is the only Vatican II document that does *not* quote papal documents).

Now, *Perfectae Caritatis* (issued October 28, 1965) does not ignore the ecclesiological turn made at Vatican II; rather, it reflects the council's ecclesiology and especially that of *Lumen Gentium*, of a church with a diversity of gifts in relation with one another and open to the kingdom. There is a clear change from the "hierarcological ecclesiology" described by Yves Congar as typical of the pre–Vatican II period, and there is an ecclesiology that makes room for the role of the Holy Spirit.

But *Perfectae Caritatis* also contains some of the limitations of the council's ecclesiology, especially in the option not to use the term *charisma* that was mentioned in the speeches in the aula during the

---

[17] See Alberto Melloni, "The Beginning of the Second Period: The Great Debate on the Church," in *History of Vatican II* (New York: Orbis, 2000), 3:91–93.

[18] See Joachim Schmiedl, commentary to *Perfectae Caritatis*, in *Herders Theologischer Kommentar zum Zweiten Vatikanischen Konzil*, ed. Peter Hünermann and Bernd Jochen Hilberath (Freiburg i.Br.: Herder, 2005), 3:512.

debate but was ultimately expunged from the texts in their final versions.[19] The uncertainty of the council's ecclesiology on religious orders is not completely different from the uncertainty about other charismatic presences in the life of the church, such as the new ecclesial movements.[20]

There is an oscillation between the council's emphasis on the baptismal dignity and its ecclesiology on the one hand, and, on the other, more traditional passages focused on the idea of the superiority and excellence of the "state of perfection" (PC 1; PC 5–6; PC 14). And there are other limitations not derived from the other Vatican II texts, especially a theology of religious life that draws on the traditional idea of the division between different "states of perfection."

What is clear in the ecclesiology of Vatican II is an emphasis on a given idea of ministry that is not part of the conciliar document on religious life: only paragraphs 8 and 20 of *Perfectae Caritatis* are devoted to ministry. What emerges clearly is that at Vatican II we have a paradox about the renewal of religious life and religious orders: the movement does not come from the religious orders themselves and not from the bishops belonging to a religious order (see the 1964 debate), but only from the whole ecclesiological debate that took place at the council. This is a key element to understanding the reception of the document and the renewal of the religious orders after Vatican II.

3. Religious Orders and Post-Conciliar Ecclesiology

The reception of *Perfectae Caritatis* must be read in the context of the reception of Vatican II in general and of its ecclesiology in particular.

---

[19] The idea of "charisma of the founder" or "of the institute" is present only and in a very tangential way in the decree on missionary activity *Ad Gentes* 23. See Yuji Sugawara, "Concetto teologico e giuridico del "carisma di fondazione" degli istituti di vita consacrata," *Periodica* 9 (2002): 239–71.

[20] About this, see Massimo Faggioli, *Sorting Out Catholicism: A Brief History of the New Ecclesial Movements*, trans. Demetrio S. Yocum (Collegeville, MN: Liturgical Press, 2014).

The very first reception of Vatican II's ecclesiology happened during the council itself, with what German ecclesiologist Hermann Pottmeyer called the "unfortunate change" from *communio* to *hierarchica communio* in the "Nota Explicativa Praevia" to *Lumen Gentium* (November 1964)[21]—a change that corrected the course of post–Vatican II ecclesiology even before all the conciliar documents were approved. The tension emerging around the *Nota* was foreshadowing, if not creating, the tensions of the post-conciliar period.

We have in post–Vatican II ecclesiological discourse a series of tensions, but also a certain history of different ecclesiological "seasons": the decentralization of the 1970s (thanks also to the liturgical reform); the shift from the "ecclesiology of the people of God" to the "ecclesiology of communio" in the 1980s (especially after the 1985 Extraordinary Synod on the reception of Vatican II); the recentralization of the 1990s (letter of the CDF *Communionis Notio*, 1992; motu proprio *Apostolos Suos*, 1998); the "universal versus local" debate in the 2000s (the Ratzinger-Kasper public exchange); the rediscussion of the hermeneutic of Vatican II with all its ecclesiological repercussions during the pontificate of Benedict XVI.

All these ecclesiological tensions overshadow another simple fact. The post-conciliar period since the 1970s, after only a few years of lasting consensus, sees a growing rift between theologians and hierarchy who had worked well together at Vatican II. It is a period when the life of the church receives the message of Vatican II but at the same time the life of the church proves and develops much more quickly in directions not foreseen by the council fathers and the documents they approved. The new role of *the laity in the church on the one hand* and the renewed role of the *bishops and the papacy on the other hand* demonstrate a lack of attention paid to the clergy and the religious. In this sense, what we can call the "post-conciliar neo-institutionalism" embraced by the magisterium (especially with John Paul II) favored bishops (the backbone of the institution) and laity (who can easily bypass the institutional mechanisms), but put in

---

[21] Hermann J. Pottmeyer, *Towards a Papacy in Communion: Perspectives from Vatican Councils I and II* (New York: Herder and Herder, 1998), 113.

a difficult situation those called to mediate between the institution and the reality on the ground, that is, the clergy and, in a particularly complicated situation, the religious orders. Stephen Schloesser correctly identifies with the functionalist ecclesiology of Vatican II (especially in *Lumen Gentium*) whatever excluded (or tried to exclude) prophecy in the church and especially female influence in the church.[22]

The religious not only have a part in mediating between the institution and the reality on the ground; they must also negotiate between clerical identity and charismatic voice in the church and in their own communities, and between institutional status quo and prophetic call in the transition from a monocultural, Eurocentric, and western Catholic Church to a truly global church, in ways that are not always charted by the texts or even by the debates of Vatican II.[23]

This situation expresses itself in the documents of the post-conciliar period: the 1978 Directives for the Mutual Relations between Bishops and Religious in the Church (*Mutuae Relationes*) issued by the Sacred Congregation for Bishops and the Sacred Congregation for Religious and Secular Institutes;[24] the new Code of Canon Law promulgated by John Paul II in 1983; the 1983 document

[22] See Stephen R. Schloesser, "'Dancing on the Edge of the Volcano': Biopolitics and What Happened after Vatican II," in *From Vatican II to Pope Francis: Charting a Catholic Future*, ed. Paul Crowley (Maryknoll, NY: Orbis Books, 2014), 3–26, esp. 19–20.

[23] See Diana de Vallescar Palanca, *Ordensleben interkulturell: Eine neue Vision* (Freiburg i.Br.: Herder, 2008); *Wind of Change. Orden am Beginn des dritten Jahrtausends*, ed. Andreas Redtenbacher and Joachim Schmiedl (Freiburg i.Br.: Herder, 2016).

[24] Sacred Congregation for Religious and Secular Institutes and Sacred Congregation for the bishops, *Directives for the Mutual Relations between Bishops and Religious in the Church*, May 14, 1978, http://www.vatican.va/roman_curia/congregations/ccscrlife/documents/rc_con_ccscrlife_doc_14051978_mutuae-relationes_en.html. At the meeting with religious superiors held November 29, 2013, Pope Francis urged a reform of the document regulating the relationship between bishops and religious congregations: see Pope Francis, *Illuminate il futuro. Una conversazione raccontata da Antonio Spadaro* (Milano: Ancora, 2015), 35–36.

Essentials of Religious Life that tended to reduce religious life to a monastic model;[25] and a year later the apostolic exhortation *Redemptionis Donum* to the religious and women religious about their consecration in the light of the mystery of redemption.[26] The publication of the new Code of Canon Law in 1983 is also crucial for the new terminology used to define the religious life in order to include the consideration of the forms of secular institutes and societies of apostolic life and the *ordo virginum*: it is the notion of "consecrated life" that is justified at the time for its rootedness in baptism, but it still reflects a vocabulary of separation, suggesting the clericalization of religious life rather than the prophetic call of the religious. "Consecration" is chosen over other options such as "sequela Christi."

This becomes evident at the Synod on Consecrated Life in 1994, which was followed two years later by the publication of the apostolic exhortation *Vita Consecrata*, a document that, while presenting some meaningful insights, basically draws from a revival of a theological approach concerning the different "states of life"—the three traditional "states" of the laity, ordained ministers, and consecrated persons—and emphasizes the theology of consecration.[27] It is also interesting to see that in the *Lineamenta* for the Synod on evangelization of 2012 the consecrated life was mentioned *after* the new ecclesial movements.[28]

---

[25] See Sacred Congregation for Religious and for Secular Institutes, *Essential Elements in the Church's Teaching on Religious Life as Applied to Institutes Dedicated to Works of the Apostolate*, May 31, 1983, http://www.vatican .va/roman_curia/congregations/ccscrlife/documents/rc_con_ccscrlife_doc _31051983_magisterium-on-religious-life_en.html.

[26] John Paul II, apostolic exhortation *Redemptionis Donum*, March 25, 1984, http://w2.vatican.va/content/john-paul-ii/en/apost_exhortations/documents /hf_jp-ii_exh_25031984_redemptionis-donum.html.

[27] John Paul II, apostolic exhortation *Vita Consecrata*, March 25, 1996, http:// w2.vatican.va/content/john-paul-ii/en/apost_exhortations/documents/hf_jp-ii _exh_25031996_vita-consecrata.html.

[28] See Vivienne Keely, "Aspects of Mission in Religious Life since the Second Vatican Council," in *A Future Built on Faith: Religious Life and the Legacy of Vatican II*, ed. Gemma Simmonds (Dublin: Columba, 2014), 81–102.

In this sense, it is striking to see the difference between th jectories of the role of the religious orders and of the new Cat movements in the magisterium during these last thirty years. The new ecclesial movements were given a substantial preference over the religious orders. But it is interesting to remember that the leaders and apologists of Catholic ecclesial movements of the post-conciliar period have been eager to be identified in their official reconstructions and foundational myths with the origins of the religious orders. During the 1980s and 1990s, the rhetoric of the new Catholic movements as "heirs" of the medieval mendicant orders, the religious orders of the early modern age, and Tridentine Catholicism (especially of the Jesuits in the case of Opus Dei, which tried to reclaim for twentieth-century Catholicism the same role played by the Society of Jesus in the post-Trent period) became part of the apologetics of the post-conciliar Catholic movements.[29]

This rhetoric allowed the movements to avoid, once again, coming to terms with the ecclesiological turning point represented by Vatican II—a coming to terms that the religious orders could not avoid. From an ecclesiological viewpoint, we can observe that certain analogies between the new movements and the medieval mendicant orders, often reiterated for apologetic purposes, implied a dismissal of Vatican II, its ecclesiology, and its overall vision of the baptized as "people of God." In an uncommonly clear fashion, the Italian ecclesiologist Severino Dianich observed that "the new Catholic groups arise from a constant spur, that is, the feeling of a fundamental inadequacy of the local church with regard to its mission and to the demands of an authentic evangelical existence. The question is, how far can we go with this verdict of inadequacy?"[30] It is now clear that this "verdict of inadequacy" extended also to the religious orders that do not have the luxury of the freedom to navigate the system of the Catholic Church with the same fluctuations typical of

[29] See Massimo Faggioli, *The Rising Laity: Ecclesial Movements since Vatican II* (Mahwah, NJ: Paulist Press, 2016), 87–112.

[30] Severino Dianich, "Le nuove comunità e la "grande chiesa": un problema ecclesiologico," *La Scuola Cattolica* 116 (1988): 512–29.

some of the new Catholic movements: between ultramontanism and neo-gallicanism, between hyperclericalism and lay empowerment, between radical openness to the world and withdrawal from the world, between democratic self-government and cult-like obedience to the charisma of the founder.

4. Religious Orders in the Church after Vatican II: A Few Hypotheses

These last few decades have coincided with a moment of tension for the role of religious in the church, and not only because of Vatican doctrinal policy. As an ecclesiologist and a church historian, I have three hypotheses for these tensions, hypotheses that try to go beyond the caricature of a simple power struggle (granted that power struggles exist in the church) but that take seriously what Jorge Mario Bergoglio said in his intervention at the 1994 Synod on Consecrated Life: "we can reflect upon the consecrated life only from the inside of the church, looking at the inter-ecclesial relations that consecrated life implies."[31]

The issue at the center of the first hypothesis is the relationship between religious and episcopate. *The first hypothesis* develops around the idea that, in order to understand the role of the religious in the church of tomorrow we also need a reflection on the *development of the relationship among church, society, and political community*, and not just an intra-Catholic analysis of the changes in ecclesiology compared to the changes in the real life of the church and of the religious. The big change in ecclesiology that had to do with the role of the religious in these last fifty years concerns the change in the perception of religious life after Vatican II. On the one hand there is the obvious consideration that the "universal call to holiness" has redefined the position of the clergy but especially of

---

[31] See Giuseppe Ferraro, *Il Sinodo dei Vescovi. Nona Assemblea Generale Ordinaria (2–30 ottobre 1994)* (Rome: La Civiltà Cattolica, 1998), 278 ("Non si può riflettere sulla vita consacrata se non dall'interno della Chiesa, sottolineando i rapporti inter-ecclesiali che essa implica").

the consecrated and members of the religious orders. Less obvious, however, is the fact that the role of the religious has been redefined by factors that are non-theological and non-ecclesiological, but social and in a sense "political." Many services provided by the religious orders in the last few centuries have been taken up by the political community and have become part of the social contract. In this sense, the hidden element in the redefinition of the religious in the post–Vatican II period is the new acknowledgment of the secular realm (decolonization and the rise of constitutional democracies, the state, the government, the welfare state) by the church at the council. The papacy, the episcopacy, and the clergy have *not* gone through the radical redefinition that religious orders had to go through: the history of the religious orders between the French Revolution and the 1905 "Law of Separation" between church and State in France is instructive in this respect.[32] Religious and consecrated *lost a significant part of their role in the church and in society and politics* and they did not get (at least symbolically) from the church nor from the secular state the "reparations" that the institutional Catholic Church (the Holy See and the bishops) got in terms of political recognition during the twentieth century.

The second hypothesis develops some reflections *on the new forms of "religious lifestyles" in the Catholic Church* in the last century and touches on the relationship between the religious and new forms of communal life in the church in light of the clerical/lay identity. The ecclesiology of the *duo genera Christianorum* was no longer normative even before Vatican II started, if we just remember the new developments for the new "secular institutes" already under Pius XI and Pius XII.[33] Vatican II underdevelops the already existing variety of forms of Christian life by enhancing the laity through the "universal call to holiness" and strengthening the power of the

---

[32] See Christian Sorrel, *La République contre les congrégations. Histoire d'une passion française (1899–1904)* (Paris: Cerf, 2003).

[33] See here the contribution of the young Giuseppe Dossetti to the papal magisterium: see Enrico Galavotti, *Il giovane Dossetti. Gli anni della formazione 1916–1939* (Bologna: Il Mulino, 2006), 205–15.

bishops by a "constitutionalization" of collegiality, thus leaving the religious orders in a difficult situation. The council's ecclesiology had ignored the specific role of the religious orders. We could say that if Vatican II—which for some is the equivalent of the French Revolution for Catholicism[34]—acknowledged the importance of freedom for the church (*liberté*) and equality of all the baptized (*égalité*), it nonetheless failed to include in the "constitution" of the Catholic Church the element of fraternity (*fraternité*) by failing, in its theology of the religious orders, to identify fraternity as the link between the society of citizens of the world and the community of men and women in the faith.[35] At the same time, the specific social role of the religious orders was increasingly taken away by the secularization of social services in the modern administrative state, in an incongruous alliance between conciliar theology and the modern state.[36] On the one side, however, the work of charity is part of the essence of the church and cannot be outsourced or absorbed by the social services of the state;[37] on the other side, the legacy of the religious orders and of the different ways of being part of a religious order did not get lost. The services provided by many of the new Catholic movements are in the tradition of the religious orders (education, formation, welfare, prison ministry, and so forth). But what allows the new Catholic movements to play the role of the early religious orders is an institutional "lightness" (the non-clerical status of the members, their lifestyle, the relations with the church hierarchy, their relations with modern culture, their social and political engagement, and so forth) that the religious orders have lost in the centralization and

[34] About this accusation, originating from the Lefebvrites' rejection of Vatican II, see John W. O'Malley, "The Style of Vatican II," *America* (February 24, 2003): 12–15.

[35] About this, see Marcello Neri, *Giustizia come misericordia. Europa, cristianesimo e spiritualità dehoniana* (Bologna: EDB, 2016), 113.

[36] On this issue, see also Walter Kasper, *Mercy: The Essence of the Gospel and the Key to Christian Life* (Mahwah, NJ: Paulist Press, 2014), 185–205.

[37] See Benedict XVI, encyclical *Deus Caritas Est* 25–28; http://w2.vatican.va/content/benedict-xvi/en/encyclicals/documents/hf_ben-xvi_enc_20051225_deus-caritas-est.html.

clericalization of the church during the last couple of centuries.[38] In other words, the prophetic and radical nature of the religious could survive better in new Catholic groups that had a different kind of relationship with the institution, also because they were "protected" by their lay status. In a church that had become, for many reasons, less hospitable to them, religious orders had to carry the burden of their clerical status and of being on the margins, or the burden of being "differently clerical" (if you allow me) but without the benefits of the freedom of lay Catholics, who now have the luxury of behaving like the clergy and the consecrated with all the benefits that a situation *de facto* and *extra legem* provides.

The third hypothesis touches on the relationship between the role of the religious in the church of today and the history of the debate on Vatican II. *Both the nostalgic defense of the council and the anti–Vatican II traditionalist mind-set prove incapable of developing a creative vision for a new role of the religious in the church of tomorrow.* The veterans' sentimentality for the church of Vatican II underestimates the weakness of the reflection of the council on the religious and the rapid development of new issues (ecclesiological and others) that require that we *begin from the council without stopping there*. The anti–Vatican II traditionalists are, on the other hand, ready to ignore that the issues surrounding the role of the religious orders were not created by the council but were there already. For the traditionalist narrative that is at the heart of the anti–Vatican II sentiment the need to preserve the prophetic role of the religious in the church is evidently missing because the anti–Vatican II narrative is largely (although not only) a "status quo ante narrative"[39]—and we all know that prophecy and status quo are not good travel companions. In this respect it would be interesting to see the relations

[38] About the different kinds of relationship between church and political power and its impact on religious orders, see Sandra Schneiders, *Buying the Field: Catholic Religious Life in Mission to the World*, Religious Life in a New Millennium 3 (Mahwah, NJ: Paulist Press, 2013), esp. 10–23.

[39] See Massimo Faggioli, *Vatican II: The Battle for Meaning* (Mahwah, NJ: Paulist Press, 2012).

between the development of the "Jesus studies" in academia and the rise of Jesus as the paradigm of Christian life in our secular age, on the one hand, and the reception of these studies among traditionalist Catholics, on the other hand, in order to understand the impact of this "new" paradigm (much stronger than institutional ones) on the perception of the religious orders in the church. Studies of the life of Jesus have emphasized the prophetic nature of his actions: his close contact with poor people, his relationship to his social environment, his perception of the needs of others as a call to service, and a dedication to the gospel in line with listening to the signs of the times. Pope Francis said to the Poor Clare sisters in Assisi on October 4, 2013 that the typical element of the consecrated is to be prophets that witness the way Jesus lived on this earth, witnessing therefore also the humanity of Jesus Christ.[40] But maybe in the life of the church, including the communities of consecrated, we are still far from comprehending the radical conversion required by the option of choosing the humanity of Jesus as a model. A definition of ministries established once and for all does not answer the needs of the mission, which should be not the description of what "we think of us" (as it is today in the corporate world), but a challenge. A lot of what defines mission and ministry in the church has changed in these last fifty years, and that is even truer for the role of the religious.

5. Vatican II, Religious Orders, and Catholicism in the Public Square Today

Is it still worth looking at Vatican II for the future of the religious orders in the church? I think it is, provided we can distinguish between what we can learn from Vatican II, what we can leave behind, and what we can reclaim and develop for the future of the church.

What we can leave behind is the intellectual neglect of the particularity of the religious orders because of an ecclesiological debate

---

[40] See Pope Francis's Address to the Cloistered Nuns in Assisi, October 4, 2013, https://w2.vatican.va/content/francesco/it/speeches/2013/october /documents/papa-francesco_20131004_monache-assisi.html.

centered on issues of power (clergy versus laity; universal versus local; bishops versus religious). The claim of the episcopacy to be the sole power holder in the church looks particularly old-fashioned today, and not primarily for theological reasons. The idea that the church is centered on the diocese and parish is something that Vatican II takes from Trent much more than is usually acknowledged. In the Constitution on the Sacred Liturgy the council spoke of the parish in the context of the theology of a Eucharistic local church, but the issue of the parish and of the parish clergy was addressed very randomly and casually. On the other hand, in the post-conciliar ecclesiological magisterium the emphasis on *communio* (at the expense of the ecclesiology of the people of God) was one of the causes of the weakening of the theology of church structures.[41] The current parish model, if it is the only model, is clearly not sustainable for the future of the church. The centrality of the parish model developed in Christendom and modern Europe as the key institution of a Catholic Church with a territorial dimension and jurisdiction that was supposed to mirror the jurisdiction of the secular, political counterpart, that is, the state. That parallelism and competition no longer works theologically or politically: the relations between what is religious and what is political are no longer defined by church and state and by geographical and juridical boundaries, and the liminal characteristic of the religious orders corresponds to the needs of the church in the present situation, provided that is not too late to recover a role for the religious orders.

What needs to be reclaimed and developed from Vatican II is much, and in particular from the new emphasis on Vatican II under Pope Francis. First, Francis's ecclesiology has given new legitimacy to the idea of inculturation related to evangelization, something that the religious are in a privileged position to do if compared with the role of the hierarchical church.[42] Second, Francis's focus is eschatological

---

[41] See Giampietro Ziviani, *Una Chiesa di popolo. La parrocchia nel Vaticano II* (Bologna: EDB, 2011).

[42] See, for example, Francis's conversation with the Union of Superiors General at the end of their eighty-second assembly in Rome, on November 29, 2013, in Pope Francis, *Illuminate il futuro*, 22–23.

and prophetic much more than ecclesiological; in this sense the eccle-siological weaknesses of Vatican II for the religious orders are going to be less of an obstacle. Third, it is a matter of institution, which the council did not reform, and charisma. Francis's reading of the council favors a post-institutional ecclesiology that works not only through the system but also beyond and if necessary without it. The charismatic element is being rediscovered after it was undervalued and under suspicion for a long time, even in the post-conciliar period. In a church that defends the poor and marginalized, it is clear that the religious orders are a prime example of a church that is not a flight from the world, but "a flight from the power structures of the Empire" of today.[43] In an evangelizing church, the role of the religious is more important than it has been: "Religious live in the revolving door of the church, figuratively speaking. We meet people on their path into and on their way from the Church."[44]

Overall, if we want to understand the Second Vatican Council and its impact on the church we have to consider its macro-shifts, and in particular the three main insights of the council as recently sum-marized by one of its most important interpreters, German-French Jesuit Christoph Theobald.[45] The first insight of Vatican II is a "genetic vision of the Christian and ecclesial existence" (connected to the auto-revelation of God in Jesus Christ): the ultimate reference for the relationship between church and society (but also between the church and its members) is the gospel of Jesus Christ, and par-ticularly normative is the "style of Jesus."[46] The *sequela Christi* finds a privileged example close to the margins, just as Jesus of Nazareth

---

[43] See Gemma Simmonds, "Epilogue I: Vatican II—Whose Inheritance?," in Simmonds, *A Future Built on Faith*, 150.

[44] Keely, "Aspects of Mission in Religious Life since the Second Vatican Council," in Simmonds, *A Future Built on Faith*, 96.

[45] See Christoph Theobald, *Le Concile Vatican II. Quel avenir?* (Paris: Cerf, 2015), 159–80.

[46] See also Christoph Theobald, *Christianisme comme style. Une manière de faire de la théologie en postmodernité*, 2 vols. (Paris: Cerf, 2007).

was a "marginal Jew" (to quote the title of John P. Meier's work)—
not only of society but also of the institutional church.[47]

The second is Vatican II's intuition of a "manner of proceeding":
the church of Vatican II is a synodal and communional church that
learns from the *modus agendi* of Christ and his *modus conversationis*. This marks the difference (but not a separation) between our
"congregating" as Christians and our life in society and the "life in
community." The style of communal living is not just an example of
a certain *modus conversationis* to the whole church (in which collegiality is severely underdeveloped) and to the world, but also part
of the unfinished business of the council (it is noteworthy that at a
certain moment in the debate on bishops and dioceses the council
was about to recommend communal living for *all* diocesan priests).[48]
The *modus conversationis* of the religious orders has a deep ecclesial
meaning, but it also sends a political message about the relations
between Catholicism and democracy: the way religious orders have
governed themselves was the start of the history of democracy, no
less than the history of conciliarism.[49] The "constitutional organization" of the religious orders has always been a great source of
institutional wisdom in the Catholic Church, and Pope Francis's
innovations in church governance, especially the creation of the
"Council of cardinals" announced four weeks after his election, are
the latest evidence of that.

The third intuition is of "a Church in history and society"—a
church that is "at the service of the Kingdom" where "Christian
vocation is at the service of the call to be human" in a "diaconal way

[47] See Massimo Faggioli, "Vatican II and the Church of the Margins," *Theological Studies* 74 (September 2013): 808–18.

[48] See Massimo Faggioli, *Il vescovo e il concilio. Modello episcopale e aggiornamento
al Vaticano II* (Bologna: Il Mulino, 2005).

[49] See Léon Moulin, "Sanior et major pars. Note sur l'évolution des tech-
niques électorales dans les ordres religieux du VIe au XIIIe siècle," *Revue
historique de droit français et étranger* 35 (1958): 367–97 and 490–529; Léo
Moulin, "Une source méconnue de la philosophie politique marsilienne :
l'organisation constitutionnelle des ordres religieux," *Revue française de science
politique* 33, no. 1 (1983): 5–13.

to express what is distinctive about Christianity."[50] This calls into question our hierarchical understanding of the church as well as what Theobald calls "all those authoritarian pastoral strategies that do not work through the charisms and through those signs given effectively to the local communities and societies."[51] The charismatic element is one of the few safeguards for a truly Catholic countercultural agenda that does not want to turn ideological.

All this considered, the ecclesiology of Vatican II is a framework for the future of the religious, and the renewal of the church in light of the council relies on the contribution of the religious probably more than the institutional church is eager to concede. What happened in the post-conciliar church was not just a weakening of the role of religious orders in the church; it was also a shift toward a church relying more and more on a new kind of church membership, that of the new ecclesial movements, which could be seen not just as the new laity, but also as the successor of the religious orders in the role of the competitors of the parish-based church. In this sense, the pontificate of Francis offers new perspectives about the role of this particular kind of laity.

[50] Theobald, *Le Concile Vatican II*, 176.
[51] Ibid., 177.

Chapter Two

Church and World in Pope Francis's Ecclesiological Shift

Evolution or Crisis of the New Ecclesial Movements?

1. Introduction

If we try to understand the Catholic Church today it is not enough to analyze the role of the papacy, of the bishops, and of the religious orders. It is also necessary, both for an intra-ecclesial perspective and for the position of the church in the modern world, to analyze the role of the new Catholic laity organized in the so-called "ecclesial movements."

The term *movement* in this context connects well the two meanings of Catholic movimentism in the last century and half: a Catholic movement with the political connotations of a social-political movement vis-à-vis the institutional status quo and political power (which is relevant for the political role of Catholic movimentism in political history, especially in Europe and in the Americas), and a Catholic movement moved by the spiritual-theological idea of the church of Christ as a movement as opposed to the ecclesial and theological status quo (which is important to understand how the Second Vatican Council came about and how it was not an operation made possible only by a few hundred bishops and theologians gathered in Rome between 1962 and 1965).[1]

[1] See Angelika Steinmaus-Pollak, *Das als katholische Aktion organisierte Laienapostolat: Geschichte seiner Theorie und seiner kirchenrechtlichen Praxis in*

More specifically, the term *new Catholic movements* identifies groups and associations such as Communion and Liberation, Opus Dei, the Community of Sant'Egidio, the Focolare movement, the Neocatechumenal Way, the Cursillos de Cristianidad, the Regnum Christi movement, the Legionaries of Christ, and others that originated and emerged within the Catholic Church especially between the 1920s and 1970s, and that are still active and present in global Catholicism beyond their country of origin.[2]

The notion of "new Catholic movements" is very comprehensive and at the same time necessarily vague. On the one hand, the identification of these new movements comes not from a theological or canonical definition of them, but from the observation of the many new and different ways Catholics (lay, clergy, faithful with a monastic and consecrated kind of *regula vitae*) give form to their Christian experience.[3] It is a new way of being Catholic, if compared with the territorial organizing principle of parishes and dioceses, different or at least reinterpreted from the community-based experience of the monastic tradition, and ecumenical in the sense of post-confessional (overcoming the confessionalization of the early modern period). On the other hand, the idea of the "new Catholic movements" comes from the self-identification of groups that formed in the church especially during these last fifty years in response to several changes in the relations between the church and secular society and among different kinds of members in the church.[4]

Deutschland (Würzburg: Echter, 1988); Yvon Tranvouez, *Catholiques d'abord: approches du mouvement catholique en France (XIXe-XXe siècle)* (Paris: Editions Ouvrières, 1988); Mario Casella, *L'Azione Cattolica nell'Italia contemporanea: 1919–1969* (Rome: AVE, 1992).

[2] For a classification of the movements, see Agostino Favale, *Segni di vitalità nella chiesa. Movimenti e nuove comunità* (Rome: LAS, 2009).

[3] About this, see Massimo Faggioli, *Sorting Out Catholicism: A Brief History of the New Ecclesial Movements* (Collegeville, MN: Liturgical Press, 2014) and Faggioli, *The Rising Laity: Ecclesial Movements since Vatican II* (Mahwah, NJ: Paulist Press, 2016).

[4] For a *status quaestionis* of Catholic ecclesiology today, see *A Church with Open Doors: Catholic Ecclesiology for the Third Millennium*, ed. Richard R. Gaillardetz and Edward P. Hahnenberg (Collegeville, MN: Liturgical Press, 2015).

We must therefore accept a definition that is broad enough to describe the new Catholic movements today: "A charismatic founder, a particular charism, some form of ecclesial reality or expression, a predominantly lay membership, a radical commitment to the Gospel, a form of teaching or training closely linked to its charism, a specific focus and a commitment to bringing its own emphasis or understanding into the life of the Church."[5] Yet it is clear that for the new movements, the issue of their theological and ecclesiological identity is complex, spread along a very wide spectrum of attitudes, with tensions between opposite elements.

In light of the fact that the ecclesiology of the new Catholic movements depends on and is part of a wider ecclesiological discourse, and in light of the ecclesiological shift made visible by Pope Francis, it is necessary, in order to understand how the role of the Catholic movement is changing,

> to analyze some of the typical elements of the ecclesiology of the new Catholic movements, focusing on a tension between different elements present in the whole phenomenon of the movements but also often within the same movement;

> to offer some reflections about the role of the movements in this particular moment in the life of the church in light of the ecclesiology of Pope Francis;

> to look, in particular, at the new document of the Congregation for the Doctrine of the Faith *Iuvenescit Ecclesia* (2016);

> to conclude with some observations on the present moment in the life of the new Catholic movements for the issue of the relationship between Catholicism and the public square.

[5] Charles Whitehead, "The Role of Ecclesial Movements and New Communities in the Life of the Church," in *New Religious Movements in the Catholic Church*, ed. Michael A. Hayes (London and New York: Burns & Oates, 2005), 18.

2. A Mixed Vatican II Ecclesiology: Membership, Authority, *Weltanschauung*, Reform

The history of the new Catholic movements begins with the "old" Catholic movement of the late nineteenth century: the papacy deprived of temporal power inspires a unified movement that counts on the social and political elites of European Catholicism to mobilize the Catholic people and pushes them to reaffirm the church's control over European societies in a period of growing secularization of culture, modernization of the economic system, and distinction and separation of political power from the power of the church. The pluralization and diversification of the Catholic *movement* (singular) into *movements* (plural) takes shape between the 1920s and 1940s with the promotion of Catholic Action as *the* movement for lay Catholics, but at the same time with the creation of other entities such as Opus Dei, the Legionaries of Christ, and the Cursillos in the Spanish-speaking world, and later in the 1950s with Focolare and Gioventù Studentesca (later Communion and Liberation) in northern Italy.[6] The third wave of new Catholic movements emerges in the 1960s during and after Vatican II and continues into the 1970s. The crisis of centralized Catholic Action no longer under the strict control of the bishops, the emergence of the Catholic Charismatic renewal, and a more militant political engagement of Catholics in movements oriented toward radical advocacy for social justice and reforms in the church are some of the elements for the emergence of the new Catholic movements in the post–Vatican II period. But also those movements founded before Vatican II go through a phase of redefinition during the post–Vatican II period.[7]

Keeping in mind the history of the movements is important for every analysis of the phenomenon, because when we try to iden-

---

[6] See John Pollard, "Pius XI's Promotion of the Italian Model of Catholic Action in the World-Wide Church," in *Journal of Ecclesiastical History* 63 (October 2012): 758–84.

[7] The transformation of Opus Dei into a "personal prelature" in 1982 is just one example of the validity of a periodization marked by Vatican II even for those movements that were founded before the council.

tify the Catholic movements today, we must remember that they are a very heterogeneous mix of different communities, groups, and associations in which the preconciliar, the conciliar, and the post-conciliar Catholic cultures coexist. This is also true for the ecclesiological emphasis within each movement.[8] Not only is the council's ecclesiology a multifaceted ecclesiology in which different models are combined and balance one another; the ecclesiology of the Catholic movements combines in very different proportions very different elements, such as Vatican II's theology of the laity, a kind of ultramontanism coming from Vatican I, and a liberal post–Vatican II approach to the issue of church authority.

The ecclesiology of Vatican II is only one of the council's most visible facets in the new Catholic movements, also because a clear tolerance for the movements by the institutional church under John Paul II was part of the "Vatican II nominalism" of the magisterium (at some point almost everything seemed to be the result of the council) as well as a certain "Vatican II nominalism" by the movements (that tended to interpret themselves as the fruit of the spirit of the council).[9] In other words, both the movements created before Vatican II and those born after it accepted, received, and appropriated the ecclesiological, ecumenical, interreligious turn of the council in different ways: for example, ecumenism and interreligious dialogue play a much bigger and different role in Focolare and St. Egidio than in Opus Dei and Communion and Liberation.

Nevertheless, all the Catholic movements are "conciliar" in the sense that they interpret Vatican II as a moment of redefinition of their role and position within the church and specifically vis-à-vis the local bishops and the pope, with a loss of authority for the local

---

[8] See Severino Dianich, "Le nuove comunità e la 'grande chiesa': un problema ecclesiologico," *La Scuola Cattolica* 116 (1988): 512–29; Piero Coda, "Movimenti ecclesiali e chiesa in Italia. Spunti ecclesiologici," *Communio* 149 (September–October 1996): 64–73.

[9] See Massimo Faggioli, "Between Documents and Spirit: The Case of the New Catholic Movements," in *After Vatican II: Trajectories and Hermeneutics*, ed. James L. Heft with John O'Malley (Grand Rapids, MI, and Cambridge, UK: Eerdmans, 2012), 1–22.

bishops and an augmented role for the papacy as the unique point of reference for their theological identity. Here the undeniable continuity between nineteenth-century ultramontanism and the new Catholic movements cannot conceal a clear discontinuity between the nature of the nineteenth-century Catholic movement and the new Catholic movements in the post-conciliar age. Here a few elements of discontinuity are worth analyzing.

First of all, the *membership of the movements* today is made up of lay people that, in terms of social visibility, differ significantly from the lay elite of the early twentieth-century Catholic movement and pre–Vatican II Catholic Action: back then the leaders of the new Catholic movements were members of a Catholic elite still recognizable in a society that was not secularized as it is today; the leaders of the Catholic movements today are recognizable within the Catholic Church, but their role means much less for society at large; the membership of the Catholic movements is more representative of the whole church and less of its social elites.

Secondly, the ecclesiology of the membership of the movements today has accepted a *new relationship between the church hierarchy and the movement* that is much more fluid and less dominated by a model of strict obedience to church authority. It is indeed an effect of the now blurred lines of demarcation, within the Catholic movements, of the old, clearly defined boundaries between clergy and laity: relevance and authority in the church of the movements is no longer given by priestly ordination. On the other hand, even the members of conservative Catholic movements have become somehow "liberal" Catholics in the sense that their obedience to the hierarchy is no longer taken for granted. We have movements still shaped by clerical culture, but in those cases it seems to be a clericalism that applies internally, that is, for the members of the movements toward the clerical members of the movement, but not necessarily to the clergy and church authorities *tout court*. That of the movements is a phenomenon marked by "intentionality,"[10] where

---

[10] Ivan J. Kauffman, in his *"Follow Me": A History of Christian Intentionality* (Eugene, OR: Cascade, 2009), talked about two kinds of "intentionality": monastic

the dynamics of obedience and loyalty to church authorities are less shaped by laws and traditions and more subject to the relationship between a particular movement and a particular church authority in a particular moment in time.

Thirdly, the overarching theme, when we talk about Catholic ecclesiology today, is the *relationship between the church and the world*. In this respect, the issue of inclusion/exclusion is one of the most complex issues that the movements have brought into the Catholic Church. The very concept of "movement" is supposedly inclusive toward a church "institution" mostly set by laws and regulations; it is undeniable that all the Catholic movements in the last century have contributed to a new role of the Catholic laity in the church. But making Catholic laity more active in particular movements does not automatically coincide with a more inclusive Catholic Church, especially at a time when issues of gender, sexual orientation, social status, and race present the church with new challenges both locally and globally. A few key issues for the ecclesiology of inclusion or exclusion are: the centrality of the founder and/or leader of the movement and their culture for the praxis of movement; the drive to rebuild Catholicism around the sociological idea of "community" vis-à-vis the ecclesiology of communion; a "spirituality of the reconquista" vis-à-vis the culture of dialogue; the nostalgia for a premodern world and a rejection of the ecclesiology of Vatican II vis-à-vis *ressourcement* and *rapprochement*.[11] The issue of "inclusive *versus* exclusive" culture of a Catholic movement has repercussions on the *ad extra* of the movement: other fellow Catholics, their local church, non-Catholic Christians, non-Christian religions, the political realm, and secular culture in general.[12] This is a genuinely

---

and evangelical. Both are historically marked by remarkable autonomy vis-à-vis the institutional-hierarchical church (episcopate and clergy).

[11] For further reflections on this issue, see Massimo Faggioli, "Inclusion and Exclusion in the Ecclesiology of the New Catholic Movements," in *Ecclesiology and Exclusion*, ed. Dennis Doyle, Pascal D. Bazzell, and Timothy J. Furry (Maryknoll, NY: Orbis Books, 2012), 199–213.

[12] About this, see Stella Morra, *Dio non si stanca. La misericordia come forma ecclesiale* (Bologna: EDB, 2015), 68–70.

new issue, if compared with the preconciliar Catholic culture in which the relationship *ad extra* was defined for every Catholic by the magisterium.

Fourth: the church-world ecclesiology of the movements also has consequences for the *ecclesiology of reform* that the movements practice within themselves. The question is how much the movements can change, that is, how a Catholic movement can stay a movement in the Catholic Church without becoming an institution unaffected by the change happening in the whole church. The nature of the fidelity of the movements to their vocation of "movement of change/renewal versus an institutional status quo" is always redefined in times of change for the whole church.[13] Here the historical example of the institutionalization of the monastic orders and of the new religious orders in the sixteenth century is an important parallel and maybe a precedent. But also the history of the preconciliar movements of theological reform is instructive in this regard, as these movements (biblical, patristic, liturgical, ecumenical) were largely absorbed by the Catholic Church as such in the theological shift of Vatican II.[14] When the Catholic Church at the council recognized itself as subject to change, the movements that contributed to that change had to redefine their relationship with the church or they were bound to disappear, that is, to be absorbed by the body of the church.

In the Catholic Church of today, fifty years after Vatican II, the movements face a similar challenge to redefine themselves. These ecclesiological issues have become much more urgent and tangible now, when Pope Francis has brought to the church a challenge to change that also involves the movements.

---

[13] For a parallel in the history of the Jesuits around the councils of Trent, Vatican I, and Vatican II, see John O'Malley, *The First Jesuits* (Cambridge, MA: Harvard University Press, 1995) and Giacomo Martina, *Storia della Compagnia di Gesù in Italia (1814–1983)* (Brescia: Morcelliana, 2003).

[14] See here *La théologie catholique entre intransigeance et renouveau. La réception des mouvements préconciliaires à Vatican II*, ed. Philippe J. Roy, Gilles Routhier, and Karim Schelkens (Leuven: Brepols, 2011).

3. Francis and a New Relationship between the Institution and the New Movements

The particular kind of relationship between the papacy and the Catholic movements shaped during the pontificate of John Paul II is being redefined by the papacy under Francis. The ecclesiological shift in the emphasis of the papal magisterium about the movements is one of the effects of the change of pontificate: despite the many differences between John Paul II and Benedict XVI, their approach to the new Catholic movements was quite similar.[15] Francis's emphasis on a more inclusive church and on the need for more unity in the Catholic Church is a new chapter in the history of the relations between the ecclesiastical institutions and these new entities. But the change in the relations between the papacy and the movements has also to do with the movements themselves, that is, it is also an effect of the crisis or stagnation in the growth of the movements if compared with the previous decades. Granted the difficulty of acquiring hard data about the membership of the movements and their spread around the world, it is apparent that John Paul II's emphasis on the movements as part of the "new evangelization" effort did not correspond to a real change within the larger Catholic community beyond the boundaries of the new movements and communities. On the other hand, tensions between movements and parishes persist:

> The flip side of the strength of ecclesial movements reveals their weaknesses. They can be elitist and absolutist about their particular mission or spirituality. They can demand excessive allegiance. They can exalt the teachings of their founder above the Gospel and the Magisterium of the church. Particularly in the United States, they can position themselves in a competing relationship with the parish. This has been a source of tension and misunderstanding, especially between the bishops of the United States and some of the movements.[16]

[15] See Faggioli, *Sorting Out Catholicism*, 127–44.
[16] H. Richard McCord, *Ecclesial Movements as Agents of New Evangelization*, http://www.usccb.org/beliefs-and-teachings/how-we-teach/catechesis

The election of Francis took place when the stagnation in the attractiveness of the movements had become visible. At the same time, Francis has redefined the classic separation "church and society" or "church and world" and sees the movements as part of the challenge to the church to reframe the relations between the *ad intra* and the *ad extra*.[17] It is interesting to note that Francis's teaching on the movements has been mostly in the form of teaching to the movements themselves. On May 18, 2013, answering a question coming from the representatives of the new ecclesial movements in St. Peter Square, Francis presented his vision of the church but also of his vision of life in a movement:

> Please do not withdraw into yourselves! This is a danger: we shut ourselves up in the parish, with our friends, within the movement, with the like-minded . . . but do you know what happens? When the Church becomes closed, she becomes an ailing Church, she falls ill! That is a danger. Nevertheless we lock ourselves up in our parish, among our friends, in our movement, with people who think as we do . . . but do you know what happens? When the Church is closed, she falls sick, she falls sick.[18]

Francis's ecclesiology of a church open to the world also extends to the ecclesiology of the new ecclesial movements. He repeatedly warned the movements against the temptation to use the small

---

/catechetical-sunday/new-evangelization/upload/ecclesial-movements-mccord
.pdf (website of the United States Conference of Catholic Bishops, 2012).

[17] About this, see Christoph Theobald, "Mistica della fraternità. Lo stile nuovo della chiesa e della teologia nei documenti programmatici del pontificato," *Il Regno—attualità* 9 (2015): 581–88 (from the lecture delivered at the University of Vienna on October 15, 2015); in German: "'Mystik der Fraternité'. Kirche und Theologie in neuem Stil," in *Barmherzigkeit und zärtliche Liebe: Das theologische Programm von Papst Franziskus*, ed. Kurt Appel and Jakob Helmut Deibl (Freiburg i.Br.: Herder, 2016), 21–38.

[18] Pope Francis, Address at the Vigil of Pentecost with the Ecclesial Movements, May 18, 2013, http://www.laici.va/content/laici/en/le-parole-di-papa
-francesco/vegliadipentecoste2013.html.

community as a refuge to which the like-minded can withdraw. The diminished emphasis, in Francis's pontificate, on the dangers coming from modernity entailed a view of the ecclesial movements as less privileged than they were under John Paul II and Benedict XVI. The movements certainly play a specific role in Francis's ecclesiology. During the homily at Mass on May 19, 2013, Pope Francis commented on the reading from Acts and pointed out "three words linked to the working of the Holy Spirit: newness, harmony and mission." Francis continued and warned against the temptation "to build unity in accordance with our human plans": "We end up creating uniformity, standardization. But if instead we let ourselves be guided by the Spirit, richness, variety and diversity never become a source of conflict, because he impels us to experience variety within the communion of the Church."[19]

The interesting emphasis here is on the role of the hierarchy for the movements for the sake of the unity of the church: the movements cannot be about *exclusivity*. But even more important is Francis's caution against the risk of building unhealthy relationships between movements and the rest of the church. Francis is very clear in letting the movements be what they need to be, but he also warns them about the dangers of "parallel journeys."[20] This represents a departure from the emphasis of his predecessors John Paul II and Benedict XVI on some kind of autonomy of the movements from the local bishops.[21]

An interesting ecclesiological element regarding the movements in the church concerns the role of the parish and the "Tridentine" territorial structure. During the pontificates of John Paul II and Benedict XVI the preference given to the movements came, especially in some local churches, at the expense of the role of the parish and

---

[19] Pope Francis, Homily at Pentecost Mass with the Ecclesial Movements, May 19, 2013, http://w2.vatican.va/content/francesco/en/homilies/2013/documents/papa-francesco_20130519_omelia-pentecoste.html.

[20] Pope Francis, Homily at Pentecost Mass.

[21] See Benedict XVI's speech to the movements of June 3, 2006, in *Insegnamenti di Benedetto XVI*. 2 (2006): 757–65.

of the religious orders. In the apostolic exhortation *Evangelii Gaudium* (November 24, 2013), the parish is given back its proper role.[22] Francis does not recommend more integration between movement and local church to one particular ecclesial movement, but to all of them.[23] In this new emphasis on the importance of the local-territorial dimension of the church there is Francis's pastoral experience in a particular urban social geography,[24] but also a renewed link between ecclesiology and the emphasis on social justice,[25] and part of Francis's ecumenical ecclesiology.[26]

The most significant shift from John Paul II and Benedict XVI is Francis's constant call to the movements to see themselves not as the elites of the church or the paradigm of a new militant church, but as part of the whole Catholic Church. Care for the unity of the church, freshness of the charism, and respect for the freedom of

---

[22] Pope Francis, Apostolic Exhortation *Evangelii Gaudium* (November 24, 2013), par. 28–29.

[23] See Pope Francis, Address to Representatives of the Neocatechumenal Way, February 1, 2014, http://w2.vatican.va/content/francesco/en/speeches/2014/february/documents/papa-francesco_20140201_cammino-neocatecumenale.html.

[24] See Carlos Maria Galli, *Dio vive in città. Verso una nuova pastorale urbana*, preface by Andrea Riccardi, founder of the Community of Sant'Egidio (Città del Vaticano: Libreria Editrice Vaticana, 2014). Particularly interesting is Francis's emphasis on the sanctuaries and his idea to reshape the parishes learning from the spiritual vitality of the urban, suburban, and rural sanctuaries (229–33).

[25] See, for example, Pope Francis, Address to the Participants in the World Meeting of Popular Movements (October 28, 2014), http://w2.vatican.va/content/francesco/en/speeches/2014/october/documents/papa-francesco_20141028_incontro-mondiale-movimenti-popolari.html.

[26] See Francis's speech to the Pentecostals in Caserta (Italy), July 28, 2014, https://w2.vatican.va/content/francesco/it/speeches/2014/july/documents/papa-francesco_20140728_caserta-pastore-traettino.html. For the reference to the "ecumenism of blood," see also the address to the members of the Renewal of the Holy Spirit on July 3, 2015: Pope Francis, Discorso al movimento del Rinnovamento nello Spirito, http://w2.vatican.va/content/francesco/it/speeches/2015/july/documents/papa-francesco_20150703_movimento-rinnovamento-spirito.html (available only in Italian, Spanish, and Portuguese).

the faithful in the movements—these three elements sum up the recommendations of Francis to the new ecclesial realities during the first two years of his pontificate. Francis offered a most complete version of his vision in the Address to the Participants in the Third World Congress of Ecclesial Movements and New Communities on November 22, 2014, with a very interesting emphasis on the care for the wounded humanity that seeks refuge in the movements and the importance of communion in the church.[27]

Francis reminds the movements of the danger of exclusivity and self-referentiality in the church—especially when belonging to a movement becomes a label:

> When we are slaves to self-referentiality we end up culti-vating a "labelled spirituality": "I'm a member of CL [Com-munion and Liberation]." This is the label. Then we fall into the thousands of traps offered to us by the pleasure of self-referentiality; by that looking at ourselves in the mirror which leads us to confusion and transforms us into mere impresarios in an NGO.[28]

Francis has evidently toned down the previous popes' emphasis on the special role of the movements, but he has not turned cold toward them. Rather, he has pointed out the possible distance between the movements' charismatic gifts and their founders on one side and their later development and real life of the movements on the other side. By doing this, Francis dares to engage one of the most delicate issues—fidelity to the founder and his/her legacy—within the life

[27] See Pope Francis, Address to Participants in the Third World Congress of Ecclesial Movements and New Communities, November 22, 2014, http://w2.vatican.va/content/francesco/en/speeches/2014/november/documents/papa-francesco_20141122_convegno-movimenti-ecclesiali.html.

[28] Pope Francis, Address to Members of the Communion and Libera-tion Movement, March 7, 2015, http://w2.vatican.va/content/francesco/en/speeches/2015/march/documents/papa-francesco_20150307_comunione-liberazione.html.

of every movement whose founders are in some cases still alive[29] or that has just chosen its first leader after the death of the founder.[30] Pope Francis as a Jesuit knows that the new Catholic movements are facing a challenge similar to the one the religious orders went through during the post–Vatican II period: the delicate operation of balancing the renewal in the spirit of the "charisma of the founder" with the *aggiornamento* required of a church in the modern world. Francis has chosen a more cautious tone that responds to an appreciation of the role of the movements in global Catholicism but also demonstrates awareness of the tensions existing between movements and bishops in some countries. On several occasions during the first two years of his pontificate Francis spoke to the movements, always inviting them to a more collaborative stance with the rest of the church, especially with the parishes.

4. From *Evangelii Gaudium* (2013) to *Iuvenescit Ecclesia* (2016)

The change in Francis's approach to the new ecclesial movements is very visible if we look at the letter published by the Congregation for the Doctrine of the Faith on June 14, 2016 (dated March 14, 2016), with the title *Iuvenescit Ecclesia*.[31] This letter rereads *Lumen Gentium* (especially chapter 4 on the laity) in light of the post-conciliar developments, especially the phenomenon of the flourishing

---

[29] For example, the Community of St. Egidio founded by Andrea Riccardi in 1968 or the Ecumenical Monastic Community of Bose founded by Enzo Bianchi in 1965.

[30] An example is the Focolare movement. The founder, Chiara Lubich, died on March 14, 2008. The current president is Maria Voce, who was elected by the General Assembly in July 2008 and reelected for a second consecutive term in September 2014.

[31] Congregation for the Doctrine of the Faith, letter *Iuvenescit Ecclesia* to the Bishops of the Catholic Church Regarding the Relationship between Hierarchical and Charismatic Gifts in the Life and the Mission of the Church (March 14, 2016), http://www.vatican.va/roman_curia/congregations/cfaith /documents/rc_con_cfaith_doc_20160516_iuvenescit-ecclesia_en.html.

of the movements in these last fifty years. But it also emphasizes LG 12, which is one of the favorite passages for Francis because of the nonsectarian "ecclesiology of the people." The letter is a well-balanced document that talks about recognizing "a convergence in the recent Magisterium on the coessentiality between the hierarchical and charismatic gifts." But it is clearly setting a new balance between the episcopate and the movements in papal magisterium.[32]

Iuvenescit Ecclesia also calls for the movements to respect the hierarchy, given that sometimes the movements have seen themselves as autonomous from the bishops. A most important passage in is the following: "When, however, a gift presents itself as a 'founding" or 'originating charism,' this requires a specific recognition so that the richness it contains may be adequately articulated within the ecclesial communion and faithfully transmitted over time. Here emerges the decisive task of discernment that appertains to the ecclesial author-ities." The document talks clearly about the right of the faithful "to be informed by their pastors about the authenticity of charisms and the trustworthiness of those who present themselves as recipients thereof." This document talks about charisma (which is conspicu-ously absent from the Code of Canon Law, for example) and is a remarkably honest document about those cases in which there is a "disordered exercise of the charisms." It talks about "coessentiality between hierarchical gifts—of their nature stable, permanent, and irrevocable—and the charismatic gifts."

The letter also gives eight criteria to discern the healthy ecclesial nature of the charisms:

the primacy of the vocation of every Christian to holiness

commitment to spreading the Gospel

profession of the Catholic faith

witness to a real communion with the whole church

---

[32] See the important analysis by Piero Coda, "Con Benedetto e con Fran-cesco. La lettera Iuvenescit Ecclesia e la 'co-essenzialità' di charisma e istitu-zione," *Il Regno – attualità* 14 (July 15, 2016): 394–98.

recognition of and esteem for the reciprocal complementarity of other charismatic elements in the church

acceptance of moments of trial in the discernment of charisms

presence of spiritual fruits

the social dimension of evangelization

Under John Paul II there was already a list similar to this one (in John Paul II's apostolic exhortation *Christifideles Laici* of 1988 and in the important pastoral letter of the Italian Bishops Conference to the movements of 1993),[33] but this new list in *Iuvenescit Ecclesia* is more cautious about the idea that new movements always bring energy and life to the church: they can also create division in the church. Number 6 will be particularly challenging for some movements: it is a realistic document that does not lie about how difficult it is for new movements to be recognized by the church.

Francis's is not an ecclesiology complacent with the status quo, and even less complacent with clericalism. The movements are a powerful counterbalance to the dominance of a clerical system. Also because of that, Francis's understanding of the word *movement* is very comprehensive: social movements and ecclesial movements both belong to a worldview in which *process* is a key word for Francis and his idea of change.[34] The world *church* as a movement is part of the transition from a modern and Tridentine ecclesial (European) self-understanding to a postmodern, postinstitutional (global) Catholicism. In this sense, one of the most radical departures of Pope Francis from the vocabulary of John Paul II and Benedict XVI about the movements and the church is the inclusion of the "popular movements" (that are ecumenical in their membership) advocating social and economic justice as an integral part of the pope's audience. This entails an ecclesiological shift both *ad intra* (movimentism is also for

[33] See Faggioli, *Sorting Out Catholicism*, 108–14.

[34] About the idea of "process" in theology and in the Church, see Francis's long interview with Antonio Spadaro, for *Civiltà Cattolica*, published in English with the title "A Big Heart Open to God" in the printed edition of *America* (September 30, 2013): 15–38.

church reform, not only for the *reconquista* of secularized society) and *ad extra* (pointing at social and economic justice resets in a non-ideological and post-European way the discourse on the relationship between Catholicism and modernity).

But there is also a deep connection between Francis's ecclesiology and the movements, in particular with Francis's focus on the *sensus fidei* and the "theology of the people." The "theology of the people" typical of Francis entails a mistrust of the elites—social, ecclesiastical, theological, or otherwise. When movements become elites in the church, here we see a clear distance from Francis's ecclesiology, in which "*communio* ecclesiology" and "people of God ecclesiology" coexist.[35] Francis considers the movements as a key part of the missionary identity of a church whose movements are part of the church as a people, where there is no elite and no lower class. Francis's messages to the movements are a clear contribution in putting to an end to the idea of the *duo genera christianorum*—"two kinds of Christians," with the movements embodying the new perfect model of being a lay Catholic in the church. Francis and the new Catholic movements share an idea of church renewal that criticizes and bypasses clericalism, but at the same time does not advocate for radical changes (such as women ordination) that are typical of the liberal culture of the northern hemisphere of the world.

Francis is a reformer, but first of all he is a "renewer." The Catholic movements of the post–Vatican II period are movements not primarily of institutional church *reform*, but of church *renewal* in the sense of a renewal of spiritual and theological culture: this difference plays a role in Francis's understanding of and messages to the movements. Francis's encouragement to the movements to work for unity in the church is part of his ecclesiology, but also of his honest evaluation of the state of the Catholic Church fifty years after Vatican II. It is his way of making clear that the ecclesiology of Vatican II and the ecclesiology of the new Catholic movements are two things that do not overlap completely.

[35] About this, see Walter Kasper, *Pope Francis' Revolution of Tenderness and Love*, trans. William Madges (Mahwah, NJ: Paulist Press, 2015), 38.

5. Francis and the End of the Narrative of the Reconquista: What Does That Mean for the New Catholic Movements?

It is not an accident that the ecclesiological document of the Congregation for the Doctrine of the Faith on the new movements came right at the end of the fiftieth anniversary of Vatican II. The years between 2012 and 2015 were not just a celebration of the fiftieth anniversary of the council but also an assessment of its legacy. Given the nature of Vatican II, this anniversary had a wide-ranging significance for the global church. Therefore it was time for a similar assessment for the history of the new ecclesial movements, whose history largely overlaps with, even if it is not absorbed by, the history of the reception of the council.

After the great flourishing of the movements during the pontificate of John Paul II, now, a few decades later, the phenomenon of ecclesial movements has changed position in the theological and ecclesial debate. Their position in the church has not changed from a canonical and institutional point of view, but the debate over them has matured and the sense of the church for this new mode of believing and belonging has matured as well. The messages addressed by Francis to the movements are the signal of a changed mood in the church about the movements and at the same time a teaching coming from a pope whose action is much more about a movement church than about the ecclesiastical, institutional status quo.

There is little doubt that from a missionary point of view the future of the Catholic Church will have to be more "movement" and less institution. The question is whether the new Catholic movements born in the twentieth century will be able to inspire this undertaking toward the future of the whole Catholic Church. In other words, it is not clear what the capability is of the "new ecclesial movements" to interpret the change in the face of the global church in the direction of greater capacity of missionary and evangelizing outreach.

The future of the movements will be about the compatibility of their different ecclesiologies with the reorientation of the church toward the world as well as toward the rest of the church—*ad extra* and *ad intra*. The new Catholic movements acquired a visible and secure presence in the Catholic Church after Vatican II thanks to an ecclesiology that spans between theological ressourcement, ecumenism, and social justice (for example, in St. Egidio and Focolare), retrieval of clericalism (for example, in Opus Dei), and the counterculturalism typical of the American "culture wars" (for example, in Communion and Liberation in Italy):[36] the importance of the movements is in the fact that they represent and embody a wide variety of theological sensibilities within contemporary Catholicism. But contrary to the contribution of the preconciliar movements that invigorated the theology of Vatican II, the history of the movements in the post-conciliar age had an impact mostly on the members of the movements, leaving largely untouched the rest of the church as well as secular society and culture. In the long run, the failure or success of the council will have an impact on the failure or success of the new Catholic movements.

Now Francis is giving new impulse to both, and it will be interesting to see how the change of pontificate and of theological culture from John Paul II–Benedict XVI to Francis has an impact on the Catholic movements. The papacy under Francis has redefined its relationship to Vatican II in terms of radical *aggiornamento*, leaving behind the emphasis on the debate on the hermeneutics: it is his way of proceeding on the path opened by the council. This means that the question of the relationship between the movements and the ecclesiastical institution, which has been managed for a long time in terms of professed obedience and personal loyalty to the pope in Rome (rather than to the local bishop), has become a serious ecclesiological issue: that is, the professed obedience to the pope is no longer able to cover and conceal the tensions between very different movements in the church because they have different interpretations of Vatican II and its ecclesiology.

Under the pontificate of John Paul II and Benedict XVI the compatibility of different ecclesiologies in the church was framed

---

[36] For an interesting exception within Communion and Liberation in Italy, see Massimo Borghesi's biography of the founder of the movement: *Luigi Giussani. Conoscenza amorosa ed esperienza del vero. Un itinerario moderno* (Edizioni di Pagina, 2015).

essentially in terms of loyalty to the papacy. But it is clear now that this equation between the Catholicity of the movements and their loyalty to the pope no longer works: the intra-Catholic theological tensions during the transition from Benedict XVI to Francis say a lot about the limits of an ecclesiology based on the identification between Catholicism and papalism. This tells us something not only about the complexity of the phenomenon of the ecclesial movements in the church, but also about the moment of crisis or evolution they are experiencing together with the whole church.

The crisis or evolution is part of the ecclesiological shift inaugurated by Francis, who has departed from some key elements of the nineteenth- and twentieth-century Catholic posture vis-à-vis modernity, thus changing the point of reference for the culture of the movements. On the one hand, for a long time the new Catholic movements were an integral part of the Catholic struggle against modernity.[37] The ecclesiology of Pope Francis is very far from the ideological pessimism against secularization and modernity that was the cultural and theological cradle in which the ecclesial movements of the pre–Vatican II and post–Vatican II periods were born. Pope Francis does not embody a liberal theology believing in the providentiality of secular modernity, but nor is he an advocate of the Catholic *reconquista* of a world lost to secularity. Pope Francis's new tone about the movements is part of his shift toward a world in postmodernity.

This changed ecclesiological, ecclesiastical, and ecclesial context provides the ecclesial movements with a challenge, which may mean crisis and stagnation of the movement phenomenon, or it may push toward an evolution of the movements. Francis's call to a pastoral

[37] In this sense it was interesting to observe the new, more dialogical tone set by the annual conference of the movement "Communion and Liberation" in Rimini (Italy) in the summer of 2016: see here the interview given by the leader of the movement, Fr. Julián Carrón, in the Italian newspaper *Il Corriere della Sera*, August 22, 2016, http://www.corriere.it/politica/16_agosto_22/carrona -cl-non-serve-nemico-comunione-liberazione-carron-meeting-c52310ce -67ca-11e6-b2ea-2981f37a7723.shtml.

conversion is a challenge for all Catholics worldwide, including the movements. The crisis or evolution of the new Catholic movements will be part of the Catholic Church's response to the challenges of pluralism and to the reactions against pluralism. The future of Catholic movimentism will be part of the bigger question on the position of the church toward contemporaneity: whether or not the church will leave behind the "culture wars," in the United States of America and beyond, in order to engage in a pastoral conversion for men and women of our time.

Chapter Three

Beyond the Paradigm
"Hegemony or Persecution"

The Church Facing Pluralism

Introduction

In his masterful book *What Happened at Vatican II*,[1] John O'Malley identifies "the long nineteenth century" with a stifled Catholic theology that was incapable of understanding modernity until very late, that is, in the middle of the twentieth century. Thanks to O'Malley, Catholics have become familiar with the expression "the long nineteenth century," a period that opened for the church in 1789 with the shock of the French revolution and did not end until after World War II—a very long century indeed.

It seems that an extension to this concept has also taken place for the political-ideological alignments within some English-speaking Catholic circles today, which may be living still in a "long twentieth century." It is not surprising that this "long twentieth century Catholicism" is responding polemically against the first truly post-conciliar and twenty-first-century pope, Francis. Among the reactions against the ecclesiology of Pope Francis, it is notable to see the quest for a viable "option" (the Benedict option, the Dominic option, the Escrivà option, the Calvary option, the Catacomb time) for the church in the secular age.[2] What all these different "options" have in common

---

[1] See John W. O'Malley, *What Happened at Vatican II* (Cambridge, MA: Belknap Press, 2008).

[2] See Rod Dreher, "Benedict Option FAQ," in *The American Conservative*, October 6, 2015, http://www.theamericanconservative.com/dreher/benedict -option-faq/, and "Waiting for Benedict," chapter 8 of his book *Crunchy Cons:*

is some kind of nostalgia for a world in which "culture" meant, exclusively, a "white Christian Catholic culture," and a nostalgia for a political and cultural hegemony that Christians in the West lost in the last few decades. All this is explained and justified with the need to exit from the mainstream and to affirm a countercultural Christianity. But as Gerald Schlabach noted recently, "Withdrawal into self-selected enclaves of the like-minded is hardly a countercultural action in our polarized society [. . .] being Catholic necessitates a refusal to leave in protest when the going gets tough, or to start a new church, or to shop around for another identity, or to bandy about threats of schism."[3]

The revival of these withdrawal options in these last few years is, on the one hand, a reaction against Pope Francis and against Francis's renewed interpretation of Vatican II. On the other hand, the proclamation of withdrawal uncovers the temptation to reduce Catholicism to a cultural option. The key issue is, once again, the relationship between the church and the world—the modern world, the secular world, and the global world—and Vatican II is at the center of this dispute around the viable future of the church in the world. In the teaching of the council the "world" is not to be understood only geographically (the new awareness of the globality and interconnectedness of the humankind) or metaphysically (the world as the earthly dimension), but also, and in a new way, in the sense of the level of human institutions that govern the economic and political dimensions of our lives in a way that is autonomous and independent from the church but not completely separated from it. In turn, the church is independent from these institutions but not completely and artificially separated. As the incipit of *Lumen Gentium* says: "Since the Church is in Christ like a

---

The New Conservative Counterculture and Its Return to Roots (New York: Three Rivers Press, 2006); Austin Ruse, "The Escriva Option: An Alternative to St. Benedict," *Crisis*, July 24, 2015, http://www.crisismagazine.com/2015 /the-escriva-option; Carl R. Trueman, "The Calvary Option?," *First Things*, July 28, 2015, https://www.firstthings.com/blogs/firstthoughts/2015/07 /the-calvary-option; George Weigel, "Catacomb Time?," *First Things*, June 28, 2015, https://www.firstthings.com/web-exclusives/2015/08/catacomb-time.

[3] Gerald W. Schlabach, "The Virtue of Staying Put: What the 'Benedict Option' Forgets about Benedictines," *Commonweal* (October 7, 2016): 11–13.

sacrament or as a sign and instrument both of a very closely knit union with God and of the unity of the whole human race, it desires now to unfold more fully to the faithful of the Church and to the whole world its own inner nature and universal mission" (LG 1).

Instead of the many options for withdrawal that are now available, there is a Vatican II option, one that we should ask ourselves if it is really part of our practical ecclesiology. In order to answer this question, it is first necessary to look at what Vatican II, the most important moment in the development of the Catholic tradition in modernity, said about the church and the world of secular institutions. Second, it is important to understand a few of the global changes that happened in the post–Vatican II period and that had an impact on the position of the Catholic Church vis-à-vis the modern world. Finally, in the context of the deep issue of this complicated relationship between the church and the world it is vital to look at the church and pluralism today.

1. The Political Cultures of Vatican II: The Church and the Global Society

One of the easiest but also most accurate definitions of Vatican II is "the event that globalized Catholicism" in the sense that it opened itself to a less Eurocentric understanding of the Catholic Church. But here "global" also means a church that takes responsibility for the global world and for speaking on a range of issues affecting Catholics and non-Catholics alike in the second half of the twentieth century.[4] In this sense, the council developed what can be called a "political culture": that is, ideas and values that derive from the Catholic tradition and grow and expand in a direction or trajectory. What are these ideas and values?

Vatican II took place just a few years after the great clash between the Catholic Church and the political ideologies of the twentieth century, and at the height of the Cold War between Communism

---

[4] See Stefan Nacke, *Die Kirche der Weltgesellschaft. Das II. Vatikanische Konzil und die Globalisierung des Katholizismus* (Wiesbaden: VS Verlag, 2010).

and the "free world." The council did not formally withdraw the anti-liberal and anti-Communist teaching of the popes of the nineteenth and twentieth centuries, but rephrased the Catholic language on the issue of individual freedom and the role of the state. Nor did it issue condemnations of Communism and liberalism; indeed, it opened itself to a new understanding of the Catholic view of the secular nation state, democracy, and individual rights, especially in the Pastoral Constitution *Gaudium et Spes* and in the Declaration on Religious Liberty (*Dignitatis Humanae*). The foundational role of John XXIII's last encyclical, *Pacem in Terris* (April 11, 1963), in opening this new chapter in Catholic theology and magisterium is beyond dispute.[5]

Vatican II advocated a balanced mix of societal self-government and government regulations. This was not just confined to the economy. It was one of the developments of Catholic teaching after the failure of corporativism in European authoritarian and totalitarian regimes, namely Italy, Germany, and Spain. It was a development of Catholic social teaching in the sense that it assumes a much more diverse world and the need for an inductive method, and it takes a balanced approach to the issue of the relationship between capital and labor. *Gaudium et Spes* (GS) spoke negatively about the Communist "collective organization of production" (GS 65), but strongly emphasized the social aspect of property and the universal destination of goods (GS 69). It spoke about fair and just wages (GS 29, 66, 71), of inequality (GS 29, 63, 85–86), of social and economic injustice (GS 9, 21, 27, 83), of poverty (GS 57, 62–63, 81, 88), and of solidarity (GS 4, 32, 57, 90). Interestingly, subsidiarity—which some Catholic thinkers today have made their most important "article of faith" concerning the government's role in the economy—is mentioned only once in this council text and in the context of the discourse on the role of the international community (GS 86).[6]

---

[5] See Alberto Melloni, *Pacem in terris. Storia dell'ultima enciclica di Papa Giovanni* (Rome-Bari: Laterza, 2010).

[6] For the use of these words, see the index in *Die Dokumente des Zweiten Vatikanischen Konzils. Zweisprachige Studienausgabe*, ed. Peter Hünermann (Freiburg i.Br.: Herder, 2012).

From a constitutional point of view, the council acknowledged the contribution of modern constitutionalism for the development of an understanding of individual human rights that is compatible with Catholic anthropology. It was the end of the Catholic theology of monarchic legitimism, of government by divine right.[7]

Vatican II talked in a positive way, even if indirectly, of the constitutions of the modern state: "In order that relationships of peace and harmony be established and maintained within the whole of humankind, it is necessary that religious freedom be everywhere provided with an effective constitutional guarantee" (DH 15, with a quotation from *Pacem in Terris*). It spoke in a positive way of the separation of powers (GS 75), of elections (GS 17, DH 5), of mutual independence between church and state: "The Church, by reason of her role and competence, is not identified in any way with the political community nor bound to any political system. She is at once a sign and a safeguard of the transcendent character of the human person. The Church and the political community in their own fields are autonomous and independent from each other" (GS 76; see also the conciliar decree *Christus Dominus*, par. 19).

This "constitutional" culture of Vatican II was not isolated from the church's reckoning with nationalism: the anti-nationalist fight of the church in the nineteenth century and the nationalist turn of European Catholics between World War I and World War II.[8] In *Gaudium et Spes*, the church acknowledged the clash with nationalism and expressed the awareness that the church had grown in that struggle: "[The Church] gratefully understands that in her community life no less than in her individual sons, she receives a variety of helps from men of every rank and condition, for whoever promotes the human

---

[7] See Emile Perreau-Saussine, *Catholicism and Democracy: An Essay in the History of Political Thought* (Princeton, NJ: Princeton University Press, 2012); Francis Oakley, *The Conciliarist Tradition: Constitutionalism in the Catholic Church 1300–1870* (New York: Oxford University Press, 2003), esp. 182–216.

[8] See, for example, Stephan Fuchs, *"Vom Segen des Krieges." Katholische Gebildete im Ersten Weltkrieg. Eine Studie zur Kriegsdeutung im akademischen Katholizismus* (Stuttgart: Franz Steiner Verlag, 2004); *"Gott mit uns." Nation, Religion und Gewalt im 19. und frühen 20. Jahrhundert*, ed. Gerd Krumeich and Hartmut Lehmann (Göttingen: Vandenhoeck & Ruprecht, 2000).

community at the family level, culturally, in its economic, social and political dimensions, both nationally and internationally, such a one, according to God's design, is contributing greatly to the Church as well, to the extent that she depends on things outside herself. Indeed, the Church admits that she has greatly profited and still profits from the antagonism of those who oppose or who persecute her" (GS 44). On the other hand, the church sees the danger of the nationalist identification of church and nation or race: "Christ and the Church, which bears witness to Him by preaching the Gospel, transcend every peculiarity of race or nation and therefore cannot be considered foreign anywhere or to anybody" (AG 15).

Vatican II clearly rejected nationalism, ethno-nationalism, and religious nationalism. The individual is protected from totalitarianism, but the council offered no critique of the modern state per se and no particular recognition of it, either. The documents *Dignitatis Humanae* and *Gaudium et Spes* speak of a legitimate public authority (DH 8, 11; GS 31, 59, 65, 70–71, 73–75, 78; see also CD 19), while also emphasizing the value of the individual and of social groups: "Citizens, for their part, either individually or collectively, must be careful not to attribute excessive power to public authority, not to make exaggerated and untimely demands upon it in their own interests, lessening in this way the responsible role of persons, families and social groups" (GS 75). *Gaudium et Spes* talks about government: "[The Church] has no fiercer desire than that in pursuit of the welfare of all she may be able to develop herself freely under any kind of government which grants recognition to the basic rights of person and family, to the demands of the common good and to the free exercise of her own mission" (GS 42, see also 79, 87). The council speaks of fatherland/country, in Latin *patria* (GS 32 about Jesus' country; GS 75 and 79 about love for the country; see also *Ad Gentes* 15, 20, 21). Vatican II takes place after World War II, but still in the middle of the process of decolonization: the nation state in the international community is at the center of the political culture of the council fathers.[9]

---

[9] See Ian Linden, *Global Catholicism: Diversity and Change since Vatican II* (New York: Columbia University Press, 2009).

At Vatican II the recognition of the nation state and its legitimacy corresponded to a strong Catholic internationalism in the form of the advocacy for a stronger role of international political organizations (especially the United Nations, but also FAO and UNESCO)[10] at the service of peace in a time of the nuclear arms race (GS 79–82). The turn from an unlimited "just war" doctrine to the exclusion of the just war definition for the use of nuclear weapons was tightly connected not only to the experience of World War I and World War II, but also to a new appreciation of individual human rights, and it will lead to a more robust relationship between Catholic doctrine and Catholic pacifism (*pax* at GS 38, 77–78, 83, 93). The trajectory of Vatican II Catholicism on war and peace has a starting point in the debate on the theological legitimization of just war, but it points to the Church's active engagement for peace.

The rise of "political Islam" is a completely post–Vatican II phenomenon, and *Nostra Aetate*, par. 3 mentions peace and freedom (*pacem et libertatem*) among the values promoted by Muslims. The political culture of Vatican II developed at the time of the decolonization of Africa and Asia, and in this sense the council's political culture was one of liberation and freedom, but in the context of the Cold War. The idea of freedom (*libertas*) has a key role in the declaration on religious liberty (especially in DH 5) and in *Gaudium et Spes*, and it is not the same idea of freedom as the medieval idea of *libertas Ecclesiae* that entails a particular ideology of the church vis-à-vis the Empire.[11]

Gaudium et Spes, par. 6 talks about "a movement toward more mature and personal exercise of liberty," but GS 20 talks about the deceiving sense of liberation offered by atheism, while GS 75 addresses freedom and political institutions, GS 88 freedom and

---

[10] For the roots of Roncalli's vision of a new international order, see Massimo Faggioli, *John XXIII: The Medicine of Mercy* (Collegeville, MN: Liturgical Press, 2014), 89–90.

[11] See Silvia Scatena, *La fatica della libertà. L'elaborazione della dichiarazione "Dignitatis humanae" sulla libertà religiosa del Vaticano II* (Bologna: Il Mulino, 2003).

the international order, and GS 92 enunciates a principle guiding the dialogue of the church: "Hence, let there be unity in what is necessary; freedom in what is unsettled, and charity in any case."

The council expressed a political culture that at the local, national, and international levels advocated inclusion instead of exclusion, dialogue, and participation (GS 9, 73, 79). It talked about the common good in terms of universal common good (*civitas* in GS 14, 20, 40, 43, 76, DH 6.13, and LG 36–37; equality in GS 29, LG 32, and DH 6).

Finally, we can say that Vatican II saw clearly the rising of a "new order" (GS 87–88 on international order, and also GS 9, 44, 68, 85, echoing John XXIII's opening speech to the council, *Gaudet Mater Ecclesia*, October 11, 1962), but with an attitude of optimism toward the possibilities opened by this new order (atheism in GS 19–21; *dialogus* in GS 40–43, 56, AG 34; *diversitas* GS 29, 61, 91–92, AA 10; *concordia* in DH 13, 15, GS 92; *cooperatio* in GS 71, 85–87, 90; evolution of the social order in GS 26, DH 1; *renovatio culturalis* in GS 49). There was awareness of ideological clashes (GS 4, 8, 82, 85) and of racial hatred (GS 82), but the outlook was hopeful. *Gaudium et Spes* calls "socialization" (GS 6, 25, 42, 75) the larger context of a social, cultural, and political order in evolution toward a system that can reflect more faithfully the message of the Gospel in a more united humanity.

Vatican II took place in a context in which Christian-Democratic parties had been or were still the leading political parties of Europe, in a moment before the great biopolitical crisis of the post–Vatican II period between church and the sexual *mores* of modern culture.[12] Vatican II expressed confidence in politics: "Great care must be taken about civic and political formation, which is of the utmost necessity today for the population as a whole, and especially for youth, so

---

[12] See Stephen R. Schloesser, "'Dancing on the Edge of the Volcano': Biopolitics and What Happened after Vatican II," in *From Vatican II to Pope Francis: Charting a Catholic Future*, ed. P. Crowley (Maryknoll, NY: Orbis Books, 2014), 3–26; Wolfram Kaiser, *Christian Democracy and the Origins of European Union* (Cambridge: Cambridge University Press, 2011).

that all citizens can play their part in the life of the political community. Those who are suited or can become suited should prepare themselves for the difficult, but at the same time, the very noble art of politics, and should seek to practice this art without regard for their own interests or for material advantages. With integrity and wisdom, they must take action against any form of injustice and tyranny, against arbitrary domination by an individual or a political party and any intolerance. They should dedicate themselves to the service of all with sincerity and fairness, indeed, with the charity and fortitude demanded by political life" (GS 75, see also GS 4, 25, 42, 59, 73–74).

2. Big-Picture Shifts in the Post–Vatican II World

We turn now to what happened in the post–Vatican II period, that is, in these last fifty years in the world in which Catholicism lives. We have perceptions, narratives, testimonies of what characterized these last fifty years, but we do not have good written histories of it. We know much better what happened at Vatican II: the history of the conciliar event has been written, and even though many aspects of it must still be investigated, there is a historiographical consensus on the main features of that event.[13] (Amazingly, this historiographical work was completed between the late 1980s and the early 2000s, that is, less than forty years after the council's conclusion. For the first real history of the Council of Trent we had to wait almost four centuries.)[14]

We are instead far not only from a consensus but also from a clear spectrum of narratives on what happened in the post–Vatican II period. In this sense, talking about the shift from the political cultures expressed at the council to the changes in the secular world of politics, in the economy and society of these last fifty years means

[13] See Massimo Faggioli, *Vatican II: The Battle for Meaning* (Mahwah, NJ: Paulist Press, 2012) and *A Council for the Global Church: Receiving Vatican II in History* (Minneapolis: Fortress, 2015).

[14] See Hubert Jedin, *Geschichte des Konzils von Trient*, 4 vols. (Freiburg i.Br.: Herder, 1949, 1957, 1970, 1975).

stepping into a minefield that is still very unexplored, at least from a historiographical point of view. (What is interesting but not surprising is that the political-theological aspect of the post–Vatican II period is relatively less unexplored.)[15]

One first major change between the perception of the world at Vatican II and what the world appeared to be in the post–Vatican II period is the degree, rapidity, and pervasiveness of *secularization*. The Latin word *saecularis* appears in five documents of the council (LG, PC, AA, GS, SC), but mostly in the sense of "worldly, earthly" and not as related to secularism or secularization. The word *secularizatio* does not appear in the corpus of Vatican II, even though it was part of the consciousness of the participants, and now it has become an important part of the vocabulary of the magisterium and theological discourse. The secular age has brought in sweeping changes for the role of Catholic education, Catholic culture, and the voice of Christian ethos in our world.[16] In particular, it has brought about changes for the role of Catholic and Christian institutions in our world and for Catholic and Christian leaders (political, cultural, and business leaders). The secular and secularization are read through the lens of Western Christendom, both at Vatican II and after.[17]

The fact that the United States, too, is becoming more secular than it used to be does not minimize the radical differences between

---

[15] See Massimo Faggioli, "Vatican II: The History and The 'Narratives,'" *Theological Studies* 73, no. 4 (December 2012): 749–67.

[16] See, of course, Charles Taylor, *A Secular Age* (Cambridge, MA: Harvard University Press, 2007).

[17] Interestingly, a recent book by Australian theologian James Gerard McEvoy points out that in Augustine "the secular" is not what it is for neo-Augustinians. Rather, "the secular" is "a common space in which members of both the earthly and heavenly cities work together in the same institutions, although for different ends, which Augustine puts in one place": James Gerard McEvoy, *Leaving Christendom for Good: Church-World Dialogue in a Secular Age* (Lanham, MD: Lexington, 2014), 152, here quoting Robert A. Markus, *Christianity and the Secular* (Notre Dame, IN: University of Notre Dame Press, 2006), 37. See also Robert A. Markus, *Saeculum: History and Society in the Theology of St. Augustine* (New York: Cambridge University Press, 1970).

the undeniable degree and depth of secularization between the United States and the much more pervasive secularization in Europe (just to limit ourselves to the northern Atlantic axis).[18] In this sense there is a difference between the church facing pluralism in a secularized world and the church facing pluralism in a multi-religious world, where the contraposition is not anymore between the Christian "free world" versus atheistic Communism, but "between those who believe far too much and those who believe far too little,"[19] or a world, as Sheikh M. Ali Shomali put it recently, apparently divided between those who do not know God and those whose faith in God makes them violent and murderous.

The second major change had to do with the development of *the issue of religious freedom.* In our cultural and political context the issue of religious freedom is connected to the rise of "biopolitics" (for example, the US Catholic bishops' fight against some of the mandates of the healthcare reform of the Obama administration between 2009 and 2016).[20] But religious liberty has become an issue typical of multi-religious and multicultural societies more than as an issue of flat denial of religious freedom to a specific religious group or church (as it was for Christians in Eastern Europe, Soviet Russia, and in the areas of the world under Communist rule at the time of Vatican II). The acknowledgment of the right to religious liberty by the Catholic Church at the council broke the ground of the acceptance of a constitutional language regarding rights and freedom, and it opened to a theological understanding of the role of freedom in faith after centuries of Christendom. The big change from the council was that the council took place in a world in which the assumption was that the privatization of the faith in a secularized society was not going to mean the definitive migration of power (political power, but also social and cultural

---

[18] About this, see *Beyond the Secular West*, ed. Akeel Bilgrami (New York: Columbia University Press, 2016).

[19] Terry Eagleton, *Reason, Faith, and Revolution: Reflections on the God Debate* (New Haven, CT: Yale University Press, 2009), 137.

[20] For the concept of biopolitics, see Michel Foucault, *The Birth of Biopolitics: Lectures at the Collège de France, 1978–1979* (New York: Picador, 2010).

influence) into the hands of the secular state (again, the issue of biopolitics) and of other non-statual, non-political entities (for what concerns the economic dimension of the human life).

The issue of the church and pluralism here is part of the tension between the idea of religious freedom as "personal freedom" and the idea of religious freedom as the "freedom of the church" to control the life of its members that might want to ignore official church teaching (see here again the debate on religious freedom and the Affordable Care Act about contraception). Vatican II advocated religious freedom for individuals and communities without taking into account that the emergence of intra-ecclesial dissent as intra-ecclesial pluralism would change the understanding not of "freedom" but of "religious": individual freedom of conscience, or *libertas Ecclesiae*: the freedom of the church *above* political power and *above* the conscience of the individuals? This understanding of religious freedom as dependent on the religious leaders of a particular religious community has also become relevant considering the role that the rise of political Islam has gained in the globalized world—remembering that political Islam was nowhere to be seen until the late 1970s and therefore not at Vatican II.[21] This has an impact on the Christian understanding of religious liberty, when often it seems that some vocal advocates of religious liberty are not really protectors of religious liberty, but just protectors of Christian liberty, that is, the liberty of Christians or of white Christians, and not of all persons of all faiths.

The third big shift that affects the church facing pluralism is the *crisis of the nation state*. On the one hand, at Vatican II there was the idea of the nation state that was either a friend or active enemy of the Catholic Church: the experience of the secular nation state that is neutral or indifferent to religion was not really part of the perception of politics at the council. On the other hand, the political

---

[21] See Gilles Kepel, *La Revanche de Dieu. Chrétiens, juifs et musulmans à la reconquête du monde* (Paris: Seuil, 1991); English translation: *The Revenge of God: The Resurgence of Islam, Christianity, and Judaism in the Modern World*, trans. Alan Braley (University Park: Pennsylvania State University Press, 1994).

culture of the council was a moment of good fortune for the idea of the nation state: it was in part due to the global polarization of the Cold War, to the decolonization movement, and to a balance (achieved after the tragic failures of the previous fifty years) between nationalism and internationalism, between state and society. What we have witnessed in these last decades is a deep crisis of the legitimacy of the nation state and what I would call the *secularization of politics*: having relied on the liberation from corrupt politics by supposedly incorrupt civil society, with results that can be assessed as mixed at best. But we have in front of our eyes a radical redefinition of the relations between power and the sacred: "In the long history of the West, the pairs 'the sacred and power' and 'church and state' were closely associated. Now they are dissociated: the sacred and power roam without borders."[22]

The original challenge to the authority of the nation state remains the church, and in a particular way the Catholic Church for obvious historical reasons. This means a special responsibility for the church and its commitment to the "common good" in the world of today. It is time to acknowledge that this crisis of faith in politics has affected Catholics as well, despite the fact that for the Catholic magisterium politics is a noble vocation (as Paul VI called it and Francis repeated).[23] This had deep consequences for the issue of pluralism if we believe

[22] Paolo Prodi, *Università dentro e fuori* (Bologna: Il Mulino, 2013), 202.

[23] "We can no longer trust in the unseen forces and the invisible hand of the market. Growth in justice requires more than economic growth, while presupposing such growth: it requires decisions, programs, mechanisms and processes specifically geared to a better distribution of income, the creation of sources of employment and an integral promotion of the poor which goes beyond a simple welfare mentality. I am far from proposing an irresponsible populism, but the economy can no longer turn to remedies that are a new poison, such as attempting to increase profits by reducing the work force and thereby adding to the ranks of the excluded. [205] I ask God to give us more politicians capable of sincere and effective dialogue aimed at healing the deepest roots—and not simply the appearances—of the evils in our world! Politics, though often denigrated, remains a lofty vocation and one of the highest forms of charity, inasmuch as it seeks the common good": Francis, apostolic exhortation *Evangelii Gaudium* (November 24, 2013), par. 204–5.

that politics is one of the ways, if not *the* most important way, to build our lives in peaceful coexistence. The crisis of the nation state is not only visible through the now long list of failed or almost-failed states that dot the world map. It is also a deep crisis of the legitimacy of politics now accompanied by the weakening of social solidarities and by the globalized financial economy replacing the power of the state and of international organizations—what Pope Francis calls "technocratic paradigm" in his encyclical *Laudato Sì*.[24]

This massive change is visible also if we look at the background of the last three popes: John Paul II had a deep sense of the nations, of their spirituality, and of their role in the history of God's people;[25] for Benedict XVI the idea of *Heimat* (which in German means the father/motherland that is not identified with the nation state) was much more important than the idea of state; Francis communicates and embodies a much larger cultural and geographical space that does not express a theology of the nations or of a particular nation.[26]

The crisis of the legitimacy of the nation state and of international/global institutions corresponds with the rise of the post-9/11 "national-security state," the surveillance state that counts exactly on the crisis of the legitimacy of politics and on the subsequent disengagement of citizens. On the other hand, there is also the rise of authoritarianism and of authoritarian capitalism in a growing disconnect between capitalism and democracy and we do not know yet whether and how it will affect the western world.[27] But there is no question that even where Christians and Catholics are a majority or a significant minority there is a deep crisis concerning the legitimacy of the nation state. In this sense I am not convinced that the

[24] Francis, encyclical *Laudato Sì*, par. 101 and 106–22.

[25] See Andrea Riccardi, *Giovanni Paolo II. La biografia* (Cinisello Balsamo: San Paolo, 2011); quite a different interpretation of John Paul II in comparison with the biographical works of George Weigel.

[26] See Marcello Neri, *Giustizia della misericordia. Europa, cristianesimo e spiritualità dehoniana* (Bologna: EDB, 2016), 26–46.

[27] See Michael Ignatieff, "Are the Authoritarians Winning?," *The New York Review of Books*, http://www.nybooks.com/articles/2014/07/10/are -authoritarians-winning/.

biggest threat to the Christian character of Christians today is their worshipping of the nation state, unless we confine this analysis to the United States, with a few caveats.[28] On the other hand, African, Asian, and Middle Eastern Catholics and Christians tend to be more appreciative of the idea of a secular state than Catholics and Christians in the United States.

3. The Catholic Church and Politics in the Twenty-First-Century World

The three shifts that I have briefly summarized for the issue of the church facing pluralism—secularization, religious freedom, and the idea of nation state—are just one way of framing the changed situation of the church in our contemporary world. The church contributed and reacted to these changes in a very complex way, and I would like here to identify a few pivotal changes and phenomena that I believe are typical of the issue of "church and pluralism."

The first pivotal change in the church was the *globalization of Catholicism* in the sense that the church is no longer dominated by a white, European, and clerical elite. Francis is the first truly post–Vatican II pope.[29] From this point of view, the year 2013 marks the definitive end of a certain type of geopolitical and geo-religious world map: a map that defined the Cold War and included a quite distinct role of the papacy as well. The election of Pope Francis represents—that is, embodies and shows—a whole new balance in the theological map of Catholicism. This did not go unnoticed: traditionalist Catholics who today reject "the new order"—in terms of economic and social exclusion, as well as of the dominance of what Francis in *Laudato Sì* called "the technocratic paradigm"—tend to place Vatican II and Francis together in one category of internationalization and globali-

---

[28] See here William T. Cavanaugh, *Field Hospital: The Church's Engagement with a Wounded World* (Grand Rapids, MI: Eerdmans, 2016), 104, quoting Paul Kahn, *Political Theology: Four New Chapters on the Concept of Sovereignity* (New York: Columbia University Press, 2011).

[29] See Massimo Faggioli, *Pope Francis: Tradition in Transition* (Mahwah, NJ: Paulist Press, 2015).

zation; they choose a traditional, preglobal church as opposed to the larger framework of a globalized ecclesial context. Their skepticism toward Pope Francis is another facet of the rejection of Catholic internationalism coming from Vatican II and in general a rejection of the ecclesiology of the council at the basis of that political culture.

The second change was a *change in the church leadership* for a church no longer deeply embedded in a Christian culture, a Christian society, and a Christian politics. On the one hand we saw the rapid deconstruction of the "Catholic ghetto" after Vatican II. On the other hand, there was a profound change in the kind of leadership the church could count on. More than thirty years ago the French sociologist Pierre Bourdieu described the shift from a cohort of bishops that he called *les héritiers* (who typically studied "secular" disciplines in secular or non-Catholic institutions and didn't feel compelled to overemphasize their Catholicism to affirm themselves in their social network, in their cultural environs, or in the church) to bishops that he called *les oblats* (coming from more humble backgrounds, less confident of their Catholic identity and their role in society, they thus dedicated themselves to the institution of the church, studying theology only, and only in an ecclesiastical setting). This change in episcopal leadership was a shift in the social background of clergy and bishops that contributed to the difficulty of the church in relating to modern pluralism.[30]

The third change is a church that has become *more plural but less pluralistic*. There are many different ways of being Catholic today, but Catholics (especially those who consider themselves true believers, especially the new inquisition called Catholic bloggers) have become less able to accept these different ways.[31] One of the pushbacks

---

[30] Pierre Bourdieu and Monique de Saint Martin, "La sainte famille" (The holy family), published in 1982 in a French journal of sociology, http://www.persee.fr/doc/arss_0335-5322_1982_num_44_1_2165 (In German: "Die Heilige Familie. Der französische Episkopat im Feld der Macht," in Pierre Bourdieu, *Religion. Schriften zur Kultursoziologie* 5, ed. Franz Schultheis and Stephan Egger [Konstanz: UVK, 2009], 92–224).

[31] See Danièle Hervieu-Léger, "Mapping the Contemporary Forms of Catholic Religiosity," in *Church and People: Disjunctions in a Secular Age,*

from Vatican II concerned the legitimacy of inculturation—theological, disciplinary, and liturgical inculturation. The issue here is the need to understand that Catholicism is not merely allowed to be plural (but only thus far) because its universalist claim is a source of globalization (this was the classical thesis). It is probably time to understand that Catholicism is plural also because its universality is also a product of globalization.[32] This means that the church has always been plural, more plural than it has been until recently, but that it also needs to learn from globalization (which entails a lot of responses to those who think about the supposedly indispensable western identity of the church and the fact that Catholicism can and should supplement the decaying western civilization).

The fourth change is in the relationship between the *church and power*, and in particular political power—what historians have called the end of the "Constantinian age" and have identified with the theological shift that took place at Vatican II.[33] *Gaudium et Spes*, par. 76 talks about a church giving up privileges; GS 40 talks about church and world united in the same destiny. The ways and times of this end of the "Constantinian age" vary significantly in this respect: also, in this case the past is not quite past. European Catholicism and American (USA) Catholicism are both orphans of their Constantine, but it seems to me that the mourning period has just started here in the United States.

In light of all this, I believe there are three particular challenges that Catholicism is facing and that are relevant to the issue of pluralism: (1) the paradigm hegemony or persecution; (2) the tension between church as community versus church in society; (3) the link between pluralism and change in the church.

---

ed. Charles Taylor, José Casanova, and George F. McLean (Washington, DC: Council for Research in Values & Philosophy, 2012), 25–38.

[32] See Nacke, *Die Kirche der Weltgesellschaft*, 40, quoting Karl Rahner, *Das freie Wort in der Kirche. Die Chancen des Christentums* (Einsiedeln: Johannes Verlag, 1953), 57.

[33] See Gianmaria Zamagni, *Fine dell'era costantiniana. Retrospettiva genealogica di un concetto critico* (Bologna: Il Mulino, 2012).

The first challenge is the paradigm *hegemony or persecution*. The church facing pluralism in our world seems sometimes to be operating under two great paradigms: hegemony or persecution. We are all aware that Christians (together with other religious minorities) are persecuted in many areas of the world. But it seems to me that in some other areas, including the United States, the church leadership is too anxious to understand the end of the age of hegemony in terms of loss of religious freedom, if not of persecution. In other words, the church seems sometimes incapable of living and operating in a socio-political situation in which there are no possibilities for hegemony or dangers of persecution.[34] It is a church that is still learning to live in the regime of freedom and pluralism in a world that is secular.

Many of the problems the church has with pluralism are part of its problems with the secular. Pluralism and secularism, secular and secularism are not identical, and in English we desperately need a translation of the French *laïcité* or the Italian *laico* to mean something like "secular, not secularist." It seems to me that many theological and ecclesiastical reactions against the secular tend to poison a possibly healthy relationship with cultural pluralism, religious pluralism, and also with pluralism within the church.

The second challenge is related to the first one and it is about a new model of relationship between the church, political power/ power of the state, and secular society. It is about *church as community* versus *church in society*, or, better, an understanding of the church that comprises both ideas: church as *Gemeinschaft* (community of personal relations) and church as *Gesellschaft* (a society made of indirect interactions, impersonal roles).[35]

In his most recent book, William Cavanaugh has clearly distinguished between "collaborative model" of the church with the state

---

[34] See Severino Dianich, *Diritto e teologia. Ecclesiologia e canonistica per una riforma della Chiesa* (Bologna: EDB, 2015), 313.

[35] See here the classic distinction used by Ferdinand Tönnies in *Gemeinschaft und Gesellschaft* (Leipzig, 1887) and later used by Max Weber.

on the one hand and "critical edge with regard to State power" on the other hand.[36] It is clear to modern theologians that a certain progress in our understanding of the Gospel has heightened the demands for those who want to protect the Christian character of the church, and here Cavanaugh is right when he critiques the blind faith in the power of the state of many Christians. But my contention here is that the development of what Charles Taylor calls "neo-Durkheimian identities"[37] (a Christian identity that is an integral part of, not separable from a national and political identity) is an element typical of a very specific portion of the Christian world—including the Catholic world—that coincides with the United States and, I would say, with an idea of the United States that might no longer exist. The crisis of politics that is developing under our very eyes seems to me a clear symptom of a deeper crisis in a certain theology and ideology of America. But again, Cavanaugh's observations are quite essential if we consider that what happened in the last couple of decades is a certain degree of "Americanization" of world Catholicism: in a sense, 9/11 and what happened since then made us (including non-American Catholics) all neo-Durkheimian, whether we like it or not. But there also, undeniably appeared a new, early twenty-first-century Catholic Americanism.

The challenge to understand the relationship between *church as community* and *church in society* is particularly urgent for American Catholics, but not only for them. This second challenge—*church as community* or *church in society*—is related closely to the kind of relationship the Catholic Church wants to have with a pluralistic world and with a pluralistic self (in terms of global Catholicism). It would be overly simplistic to characterize this issue as a dilemma between the sectarianism of a Catholicism turned community (*Gemeinschaft*) and between a purely social Catholicism turned *Gesellschaft*.

The problem is, on the one hand, that Catholicism at Vatican II made a clear turn from the church as *Gegengesellschaft*, as a counter-society, as a *societas perfecta*, to the church of the *Weltgesellschaft*,

---

[36] See Cavanaugh, *Field Hospital*, 130ss.
[37] See Taylor, *A Secular Age*, 515.

a church that is in world society and in dialogue with it.[38] It seems to me that the attempt to see the church only as a community, as a *Gemeinschaft*, carries clearly within itself the risk of recreating a church as *Gegengesellschaft*, a counter-society, in the illusion that the church as a community can be immune from corruption. On the one hand, the recent experience with the sex abuse scandal tells us a very different story about how the Christian character of the church can be defended. On the other, I believe that the idea of a church in *Weltgesellschaft* is more capable of reinterpreting the secular as a common space in which the church and humanity can walk in solidarity.

The third challenge has to do with *pluralism and change in the church*. Much of what is happening in the Catholic Church today with Pope Francis is a redefinition of its catholicity in terms of *universa ecclesia* and not in terms of *universalism*.[39] Francis's decision to have a "synodal process" with the two synods of October 2014 and October 2015 displayed the ecclesiological vision of this pontificate. It is no longer a church that pretends to be in absolute agreement on everything, but a church that admits that there are disagreements on important issues (such as the pastoral care of family and marriage) and decides to address these disagreements with a *process* that is *synodal* and leads to *spiritual discernment*. These three elements—*process*, *synodality*, and *spiritual discernment*—are not just Francis's recovery of long forgotten elements for church government, but they also constitute a reminder to our political environment that politics is a process (much messier than the absolutes of the uncompromising), is synodal (in a clear distancing from the rising tide of authoritarianism in our world), and is shaped by spiritual discernment (and not by special interests).

The Catholic Church is one of the last institutions on earth that is resisting the temptation to turn its "people" into an "audience." Pope Francis's emphasis on synodality is also trying to avoid what

---

[38] See Nacke, *Die Kirche der Weltgesellschaft*, 42.

[39] About this, see Stella Morra, *Dio non si stanca. La misericordia come forma ecclesiale* (Bologna: EDB, 2015).

is happening to secular democracies: contempt for the elites and the popularity of populists. In other words, what is happening in the church of Francis, with his emphasis on synodality here, has a profound potential for the church dealing with pluralism as well as for the church as an example for our political institutions in crisis. Diversity without unity is hardly capable of bearing fruit; but a unity that is not *e pluribus*, a unity that is not coming from diversity, is a meaningless unity. The church needs to learn an ethics of otherness in a world of pluralism in which the emphasis is on identity.

There is not just a problem of "identity politics" in the secular society. There is a problem of "identity theology" within Catholicism, a symptom of a "cultural turn" within Catholicism, which I find dangerous on many levels.[40] Discernment in a synodal process is something new we are trying for now at the level of the pope and the bishops, but it will have to spread to all the levels in the church. Handling in a synodal way the issue of pluralism within the church is important for the church, as a witness of a God who challenges all identitarian obsessions. But it is important also for our world that looks at the church with a glimpse of hope, trying to see if in dealing with this universe of diversities, Christians can succeed where others are failing.

[40] On the idea of "culture," see Terry Eagleton, *Culture* (New Haven, CT: Yale University Press, 2016) and *Culture and the Death of God* (New Haven, CT: Yale University Press, 2015).

Chapter Four

Prophetic Church and Established Church

Pope Francis and the Legacy of the Constantinian Age

Introduction

The Catholic Church has a rich history in its dealing with the past and the perils of nostalgia. Far from being an exclusively post–Vatican II phenomenon, even in the pre–Vatican II period Catholicism had to deal with the fact that the church was losing, and had already been losing for quite some time, political power and wealth, cultural influence and prestige, the role of chaplain of western civilization in a rapidly shifting geopolitics of religions.

It is therefore not surprising that a significant part of the historiographical and ecclesiological debate within Catholicism during the last century was focused around the legacy of the Constantinian age in the church and especially on Eurocentric Catholicism embedded in a system of established churches. That was one of the many ways for a still Eurocentric Catholicism to learn how to leave behind the close and exclusive association between Europe and the Christian faith as well as a particular kind of relationship between Christianity and political power.

We are now in a new phase of that globalization of Catholicism and it is time to reconsider that debate and its meaning for the church of today.

"Constantinian age/Constantinianism" and "established church" are not the same thing. By "established church" we can assume the establishment of a particular church, which is from a legal and constitutional standpoint the national church that receives special privileges (a special juridical status and financial support, among others) from the state. By "Constantinianism" we can mean a theological-political model of relationship between political and religious power in terms of alliance that is both religious and political. It is an alliance that takes many different forms and shapes in history, and it provides both parties a definite constellation of theological and spiritual ideas, political convictions and mind-sets, institutional structures and juridical language—a constellation that became normative (in different forms in different countries and geographical areas) for European Christianity for fifteen centuries, roughly from the fourth to the nineteenth century. It is a system in which political power puts the power of the empire/state and its legal arsenal at the service of the church with the church's full agreement and support: from the emperors Constantine and Theodosius in the fourth century to the Byzantine (and later Tsarist Russia) *symphonia* between the church and the state in Eastern Europe, to medieval Christendom (in Latin: *christianitas*), to Martin Luther's "two kingdoms" doctrine, to nineteenth- and twentieth-century Catholic *ius publicum ecclesiasticum* in reaction against modern constitutionalism.[1]

The theological shift of Vatican II put an end to the theological legitimacy of that constellation of ideas, laws, and practices, and started a long (and unfinished) process of institutional conversion from an institutional church of European Christendom to a missionary church. The intent of this chapter is not to rediscuss the end of Christendom, theologically or historically, nor even to explore the differences between the theological-political and ideological model (Constantinianism) and the legal system that went beyond the boundaries of Europe (established church), nor to look at the evolution of the relationship between the theological-political and

---

[1] See *Costantino I. Una enciclopedia sulla figura, il mito, la critica e la funzione dell'imperatore del cosiddetto editto di Milano, 313–2013*, 3 vols., ed. Alberto Melloni (Rome: Enciclopedia Italiana, 2013).

ideological model and the many different versions of established church in modern Christianity.[2]

Rather, the intent of these reflections is more limited: to look back briefly at the discussion and at the attitude of the institutional church toward the idea of the end of the Constantinian age in the pre–Vatican II period, and to examine how Vatican II deals with the legacy of Constantinianism.

This is necessary in order to develop some thoughts concerning the post–Vatican II period around the dilemma of the church in the age of "the technocratic paradigm" that "tends to dominate economic and political life."[3] Is the church one of the last resistants against this paradigm? If this is true, should the church let go of the established system, a system that grants the church financial support and other special privileges, if this system allows the church to provide our world with the last defense for the poor and the marginalized?

Also because of the impact of the pontificate of Pope Francis on the debate about church and political power, this reflection will focus on the case of the Roman Catholic Church. This will not necessarily simplify this analysis. There are different situations for the Catholic Church in the world in which Catholics are either the majority or a substantial minority: at the two extremes, there are countries in which the Catholic Church enjoys the favor given by the Concordats signed in the first half of the twentieth century (Italy and Germany especially), and there are countries in which there is a constitutional system of separation between church and State (such as in France and in the United States—two very different kinds of separationist models).

---

[2] About this, see Hervé Legrand, "Introduction. L'articulation entre annonce de l'Évangile, morale et législations civiles à l'ère post-constantinienne," in *Évangile, moralité et lois civiles. Gospel, Morality, and Civil Law*, ed. Joseph Famerée, Pierre Gisel, Hervé Legrand (Zurich: LIT, 2016), esp. 23–34. See also the essay by Giuseppe Ruggieri, "Évangile, morale et lois civiles. Changements de paradigm," in the same volume, 167–84.

[3] See Pope Francis, encyclical *Laudato Sì* (May 24, 2015), par. 109. For Francis's view of "technocratic paradigm" and its impact on anthropocentrism, see par. 101–36.

I am aware that the established church model in the modern period (the form it took thanks to the Concordats and part of the solution to nationalism and the rise of the nation state in the nineteenth century) is in crisis. The model of the established church is approaching its end: on the one hand, there is secularization and the end of the identification between church and nation given the sociological weakening of the Catholic Church, the impact of multiculturalism, the diversification of the religious and ethnic components within each nation, and the fragmentation of the once unified Catholic Church within itself; on the other hand, there is the crisis of the nation state that deprives the church of a partner of the legitimacy that is required in forging the alliance between throne and altar.[4]

But it is not clear when and how the established church model will end. Moreover, and this is the issue, it is not clear if it is necessarily a good thing that it will end, given the alternatives.

I cannot emphasize enough that I do *not* advocate for a return to the political and religious ideology of Constantinianism,[5] nor do I have in mind something similar to a "new Christendom" for a social and political reestablishment of the Catholic Church. Rather, I want to explore how the change in the situation of the church can influence our understanding of "Constantinianism" and of the "established church" model as a church enjoying a particular and privileged position in the constitutional order of the State.

1. The Constantinian Age in the Early Twentieth Century

The debate on the Constantinian age is a turning point in the theological and ecclesiological debate in the first half of the twentieth century. In a fine book published a few years ago, Italian-German

---

[4] About this, see Paolo Prodi, *Università dentro e fuori* (Bologna: Il Mulino, 2013), esp. 195–212.

[5] About this, see Peter J. Leithart, who calls "root-and-branch rejection of 'Constantinianism' or 'Christendom' doubly wrong-headed," also because of global Christianity's ongoing shift to the South: Peter J. Leithart, *Defending Constantine: The Twilight of an Empire and the Dawn of Christendom* (Downers Grove, IL: IVP Academic, 2010), 12.

historian Gianmaria Zamagni reconstructs the genesis of the historiographical and theological argument against Constantinianism.[6]

The thirty years before Vatican II are marked by the reflection on the crisis of Constantinianism. In 1932, in the first volume of the *Kirchliche Dogmatik*, Karl Barth identified Constantine as the reason for the decline of Christianity. In the spring of 1963 in the Rome of the Second Vatican Council, Marie-Dominique Chenu gave a paper about "The Church and the World" regarding the debate on the future constitution *Gaudium et Spes*. Barth and Chenu were not two isolated and eminent cases. The pre–Vatican II debate about the church and the world and about the legacy of Christendom also saw engaged Friederich Heer, Erik Peterson, Ernesto Buonaiuti, Etienne Gilson, Jacques Maritain, and Emmanuel Mounier, among others.[7] It was a debate that picked up traces going back to late nineteenth-century and early twentieth-century *Religionswissenschaft*: in his 1963 volume *The Conflict between Paganism and Christianity in the Fourth Century*, Arnaldo Momigliano goes back to the groundbreaking intuitions of Harnack and Troeltsch about the gap between Jesus' message and the church.[8]

A significant difference between the debate of the late nineteenth century and the 1930s is the political context. The debate about Christendom and Constantinianism between the 1930s and Vatican II was more influenced by Hitler and Mussolini than by Constantine himself,

---

[6] Gianmaria Zamagni, *Fine dell'era costantiniana. Retrospettiva genealogica di un concetto critico* (Bologna: Il Mulino, 2012), 11–19. See also the updated, German edition of the book: *Das "Ende des konstantinischen Zeitalters" und die Modelle aus der Geschichte für eine "Neue Christenheit". Eine religionsgeschichtliche Untersuchung* (Freiburg i.Br.: Herder, 2016).

[7] Barth was renewing a position against Constantinianism already visible in the eighteenth century: Wilhelm Schneemelcher, "Konstantinisches Zeitalter," in *Theologische Realenzyklopädie* (Berlin/New York: De Gruyter, 1990), 19:501–3.

[8] See also Gianmaria Zamagni, "Theology and History: A Retrospective on the 'End of the Constantinian Era' in the Works of F. Heer, E. Buonaiuti and E. Peterson," in *Pagans and Christians in the Roman Empire: The Breaking of a Dialogue*, ed. Rita Lizzi Testa (Münster: LIT, 2011), 69–90.

and it is impossible to understand this debate outside the great cultural crisis within European Christianity starting in the 1930s.[9] The most interesting advocates of the end of the "Constantinian age" were the victims of the political-theological system that led first to the alliance between the church and the political status quo and later to the alliance between the church and Fascism (in its different versions in different European countries): Heer was under suspicion,[10] Peterson marginalized, Momigliano exiled, Buonaiuti excommunicated, Maritain exiled, Chenu and Congar silenced (and the list could go on and on). In that period Christianity was split (a split with, in the middle, an enormous gray area of different kinds of consensus with the authoritarian regimes) between an institutional church allied with the authoritarian and totalitarian regimes, and a confessing church that rejected that compromise with Fascism and Nazism.

It was a split that helped renew theology. The intellectual survival of those persecuted by the church and the state defending that arrangement, and their not leaving the church while patiently waiting for better times, was one of the most important factors for the development of Vatican II. It is a debate that has an influence not only on the council but also on its reception. One of the master narratives of Vatican II is about the council that put to an end the close relationship between Catholicism and Christendom. The influence of Marie-Dominique Chenu and of the "end of Constantinianism" is undeniable not only on Vatican II, but also especially on its interpreters and historians.[11]

2. The Ambivalence of Vatican II

In fact, the position of Vatican II vis-à-vis Constantinianism and the established church is more complex. Many of the bishops and theolo-

---

[9] See Renato Moro, *La formazione della classe dirigente cattolica (1929–1937)* (Bologna: Il Mulino, 1979).

[10] See Zamagni, *Fine dell'era costantiniana*, esp. 70–72.

[11] See *Une école de théologie: le Saulchoir*, with essays by Giuseppe Alberigo, Etienne Fouilloux, Jean Ladrière, Jean-Pierre Jossua, and Marie-Dominique Chenu, preface by René Rémond (Paris: Cerf, 1985).

gians at the council, especially the bishops and theologians of the so-called "progressive majority" (with the notable exception of France), were coming from European countries with established Catholic churches.[12] On the other hand, important groups of the traditionalists and of the conservative and curial opposition to the majority came from established Catholic countries as well (especially Italy, Spain, and Latin America).[13]

The period of preparation for the Council saw the schema on the church (*De ecclesia*) building an ecclesiology that took for granted the permanent situation of the established church.[14] But the "acceleration" in the debate on religious liberty (thanks to the role of the new Secretariat for Christian Unity on the one side)[15] and the emerging magisterial contribution on human rights (thanks to John XXIII and the debate on the future *Gaudium et Spes*, with a key moment in April 1963 thanks to the encyclical *Pacem in Terris*), were a first disruption in the ecclesiological and juridical model of the established church.[16]

[12] See Michel Fourcade, "Vatican II dans le débat théologico-politique français," in *La France et le Concile Vatican II*, ed. Bernard Barbiche et Christian Sorrel (Paris: Peter Lang, 2013), 101–26.

[13] See Philippe Roy-Lysencourt, *Les Membres du Coetus Internationalis Patrum au Concile Vatican II. Inventaire des interventions et souscriptions des adhérents et sympathisants. Liste des signataires d'occasion et des théologiens*, Instrumenta Theologica 37 (Leuven: Peeters, 2014).

[14] See Riccardo Burigana, "Progetto dogmatico del Vaticano II: la commissione teologica preparatoria (1960–1962)," in *Verso il concilio Vaticano II (1960–1962). Passaggi e problemi della preparazione conciliare*, ed. Giuseppe Alberigo and Alberto Melloni (Genoa: Marietti, 1993), 141–206, esp. 188–91.

[15] See Silvia Scatena, *La fatica della libertà. L'elaborazione delle dichiarazione "Dignitatis humanae" sulla libertà religiosa del Vaticano II* (Bologna: Il Mulino, 2004), 21–42.

[16] About *Gaudium et Spes*, see Yves Congar, "Église et monde dans la perspective de Vatican II," in *L'Église dans le monde de ce temps*, ed. Yves Congar and Michel Peuchmaurd (Paris: Cerf, 1967), 3:15–41, especially for the rupture with political Augustinianism and its subordination of the temporal order to the supernatural.

The council opened on tone that differed strikingly from the official preparatory documents with John XXIII's opening address *Gaudet Mater Ecclesia*, when John addressed the topic of the agenda of the council in an historical way, talking in a hopeful way about the future, about a "new order of human relations." More important, just a few lines below the famous passage against "the prophets of gloom" there was an important paragraph about the relations between the church and political power:

> It suffices to leaf even cursorily through the pages of ecclesi-astical history to note clearly how the Ecumenical Councils themselves, while constituting a series of true glories for the Catholic Church, were often held to the accompaniment of most serious difficulties and sufferings because of the undue interference of civil authorities. The princes of this world, indeed, sometimes in all sincerity, intended thus to protect the Church. But more frequently this occurred not with-out spiritual damage and danger, since their interest therein was guided by the views of a selfish and perilous policy. In this regard, we confess to you that we feel most poignant sorrow over the fact that very many bishops so dear to us are noticeable here today by their absence, because they are imprisoned for their faithfulness to Christ, or impeded by other restraints.[17]

John XXIII set a new tone for the ecclesiology of Vatican II: not just for the fact that "the Spouse of Christ prefers to make use of the medicine of mercy rather than that of severity"—the church of mercy being something different from the "law and order" kind of Catholicism of Constantinian Christendom—but also for the pope's emphasis on the unity of Catholics, of Christians, and of

---

[17] John XXIII, opening address of Vatican II, *Gaudet Mater Ecclesia* (October 11, 1962) (translation from *The Documents of Vatican II*, ed. Walter M. Abbott [New York: Guild Press, 1966], 713). For a global interpretation of *Gaudet Mater Ecclesia*, see Giuseppe Alberigo, *Dalla laguna al Tevere. Angelo Giuseppe Roncalli da S. Marco a San Pietro* (Bologna: Il Mulino, 2000), 157–90.

non-Christians in what was a challenge to the system that divided the established church between Catholics and non-Catholics. Roncalli's attitude toward Italian politics before becoming pope was in this sense instructive and his opening speech not a total rupture from the Roncalli we know before the election to the papacy.[18]

The first message approved by the council, the *Message to the World* of October 20, 1962, contained the beginning of what *Gaudium et Spes* would develop at the end of the council, that is, the idea of a church that is engaged in the world but not protected by political power:

> It is far from true that because we cling to Christ we are diverted from earthly duties and toils. On the contrary, faith, hope, and the love of Christ impel us to serve our brothers, thereby patterning ourselves after the example of the Divine Teacher, who "came not to be served but to serve" (Mt. 20:28). Hence, the Church too was not born to dominate but to serve. He laid down His life for us, and we too ought to lay down our lives for our brothers (1 Jn. 3:16).

But it is not an ecclesiology for a church in withdrawal. On the contrary, it denounces injustices and renews its commitment for a new order:

> The Supreme Pontiff also pleads for social justice. The teaching expounded in his encyclical *Mater et Magistra* clearly shows that the Church is supremely necessary for the modern world if injustices and unworthy inequalities are to be denounced, and if the true order of affairs and of values is to be restored, so that man's life can become more human according to the standards of the gospel.[19]

---

[18] About this, see Massimo Faggioli, *John XXIII: The Medicine of Mercy* (Collegeville, MN: Liturgical Press, 2014), 99–102, referring to Roncalli's diaries when he was Patriarch of Venice (1953–1958).

[19] Vatican II, *Message to the World*, in *Acta Synodalia Sacrosancti Concilii Oecumenici Vaticani II*, cura et studio Archivi Concilii Oecumenici Vaticani,

After the opening with *Gaudet Mater Ecclesia* and the council fathers' *Message to the World*, the prophetic stance of the church at Vatican II had to submit to a debate about the "constitutionalization" of its "hierarcology" (to use Yves Congar's famous definition). In the ecclesiological debate of the second session in October 1963 the debate at Vatican II had its highest point, but mostly on internal issues (sacramentality of the bishops, episcopal collegiality, and restoration of the permanent diaconate) in a move toward a system similar to a constitutional ecclesiology compatible with the established church system—an ecclesiology that would leave on the margins, for example, the prophetic element in the Church.

In the second intersession and the third session the commission *de episcopis* debated the reform of the bishops' appointment—a typical element of the established church—before the Secretariat of State stopped further discussions on the subject: a return to the procedures of the early church for the appointment of bishops (a bigger role for the local church and its laity, a more decentralized procedure) could have jeopardized not only the clergy-dominated system running the Church but also the role of the Holy See in defending the freedom of the church in the Communist world. In the same period the Holy See was dealing with Communist-ruled Hungary to keep its privileges in the appointment of bishops for a church facing Communism, and keeping a Concordat even with Communist Hungary.[20]

The challenge to the established church system was coming from another front, namely, the debate on religious liberty of September 1964 and September 1965, which was the beginning of the end of the teaching that "error has no rights."[21] During the last session the debate on war and peace was another instance of the ramifications of the theology of the established church, notably of the idea of "just

---

vols. 1–6 in 33 books (Vatican City: Typis Polyglottis Vaticanis, 1970–99), vol. 1, no. 1, 230–32.

[20] See Massimo Faggioli, *Il vescovo e il concilio. Modello episcopale e aggiornamento al Vaticano II* (Bologna: Il Mulino, 2005), 401–2.

[21] See Scatena, *La fatica della libertà.*

war"—a debate and a final vote in which paradoxically the patriotic "established" Catholic position about the moral legitimacy of the nuclear weapons was embodied by the bishops of the United States.[22]

Lumen Gentium did not address the issue of the established church directly, even though the episcopalist ecclesiology of the Constitution on the Church leads toward an institutional ecclesiology that reflects a juridical ecclesiology coming from the experience of the established church in the modern period no less than from the patristic model of the early centuries. Other documents, especially *Gaudium et Spes*, addressed more directly the issue of the "Constantinian age." The Pastoral Constitution on the Church in the Modern World, the last document approved by Vatican II and inspired by French theology and by Chenu in a particular way,[23] opened with a statement about the relationship between the church and power: "Inspired by no earthly ambition, the Church seeks but a solitary goal: to carry forward the work of Christ under the lead of the befriending Spirit. And Christ entered this world to give witness to the truth, to rescue and not to sit in judgment, to serve and not to be served" (GS 3). Even clearer were the texts in chapter 4 on the life of the political community:

> The political community and public authority are founded on human nature and hence belong to the order designed by God, even though the choice of a political regime and the appointment of rulers are left to the free will of citizens. It follows also that political authority, both in the community as such and in the representative bodies of the state, must always be exercised within the limits of the moral order and directed toward the common good—with a dynamic concept

[22] See Giovanni Turbanti, *Un concilio per il mondo moderno. La redazione della costituzione pastorale "Gaudium et Spes" del Vaticano II* (Bologna: Il Mulino, 2000); John W. O'Malley, *What Happened at Vatican II* (Cambridge, MA: Belknap Press, 2008), 265–66.

[23] See Giovanni Turbanti, "Il ruolo del p. D. Chenu nell'elaborazione della costituzione Gaudium et Spes," in *Marie-Dominique Chenu: Moyen-Âge et modernité* (Paris: Le Saulchoir, 1997), 173–212.

of that good—according to the juridical order legitimately established or due to be established. When authority is so exercised, citizens are bound in conscience to obey. Accordingly, the responsibility, dignity and importance of leaders are indeed clear. But where citizens are oppressed by a public authority overstepping its competence, they should not protest against those things which are objectively required for the common good; but it is legitimate for them to defend their own rights and the rights of their fellow citizens against the abuse of this authority, while keeping within those limits drawn by the natural law and the Gospels. (GS 74)

Gaudium et Spes liquidated the legacy of many of the political regimes that backed established Catholicism (such as Spain under the dictatorship of Franco until his death in 1975): "It is inhuman for public authority to fall back on dictatorial systems or totalitarian methods which violate the rights of the person or social groups" (GS 75). Even clearer was the following paragraph about Catholics and pluralistic society:

It is very important, especially where a pluralistic society prevails, that there be a correct notion of the relationship between the political community and the church, and a clear distinction between the tasks which Christians undertake, individually or as a group, on their own responsibility as citizens guided by the dictates of a Christian conscience, and the activities which, in union with their pastors, they carry out in the name of the church. The church, by reason of her role and competence, is not identified in any way with the political community nor bound to any political system. She is at once a sign and a safeguard of the transcendent character of the human person. The church and the political community in their own fields are autonomous and independent from each other. Yet both, under different titles, are devoted to the personal and social vocation of the same men. The more that both foster sounder cooperation between themselves with due consideration for the circumstances of time and place, the more effective will their service be exercised for the good of all. For man's horizons are not limited only to the temporal order; while living in the context of human history, he preserves intact his eternal vocation. The Church, for her part, founded on the love of the Redeemer, contributes toward the reign of justice and charity within the borders of a nation and between nations. By preaching the truths of the Gospel, and bringing to bear on all fields of human endeavor the light of her doctrine and of a Christian witness, she respects and fosters the political freedom and responsibility of citizens. (GS 76)

Together with *Gaudium et Spes*, the Declaration on Religious Liberty (*Dignitatis Humanae*) offered a theological perspective on the issue of church and state by espousing the idea of religious liberty as a fundamental right, in a mortal blow to the idea of established Catholicism as it had existed in some European countries (Spain and Italy especially). Its first paragraph stated: "The truth cannot impose itself except by virtue of its own truth, as it makes its entrance into the mind at once quietly and with power. Religious freedom, in turn, which men demand as necessary to fulfill their duty to worship God, has to do with immunity from coercion in civil society. Therefore it leaves untouched traditional Catholic doctrine on the moral duty of men and societies toward the true religion and toward the one Church of Christ" (DH 1).

Dignitatis Humanae 5 talked about the right of parents to free choice of school ("the rights of parents are violated, if their children are forced to attend lessons or instructions which are not in agreement with their religious beliefs, or if a single system of education, from which all religious formation is excluded, is imposed upon all"). But it was the next paragraph that addressed the issue of established church most directly:

The protection and promotion of the inviolable rights of man ranks among the essential duties of government. Therefore government is to assume the safeguard of the religious freedom of all its citizens, in an effective manner, by just laws and by other appropriate means. Government is also to help create conditions favorable to the fostering of religious life, in order that the people may be truly enabled to exercise their religious rights and to fulfill their religious duties, and also in order that society itself may profit by the moral qualities of justice and peace which have their origin in men's faithfulness to God and to His holy will. If, in view of peculiar circumstances obtaining among peoples, special civil recognition is given to one religious community in the constitutional order of society, it is at the same time imperative that the right of all citizens and religious communities to religious freedom should be recognized and made effective in practice. Finally, government is to see to it that equality of citizens before the law, which is itself an element of the common good, is never violated, whether openly or covertly, for religious reasons. Nor is there to be discrimination among citizens. (DH 6)

Dignitatis Humanae did not eliminate the possibility of "special civil recognition [being] given to one religious community in the constitutional order of society," but it said that it has to be respectful of the religious freedom of other groups and of equality of citizens under the law.

Even more nuanced was the text of the Decree on the Pastoral Office of Bishops (*Christus Dominus*), which during the debate also addressed the issue of the freedom of the church in appointing bishops and the issue of the Concordats. Here it speaks of freedom of the church but also collaboration with the civil authority:

In discharging their apostolic office, which concerns the salvation of souls, bishops per se enjoy full and perfect freedom and independence from any civil authority. Hence, the exercise of their ecclesiastical office may not be hindered, directly or indirectly, nor may they be forbidden to communicate freely with the Apostolic See, or ecclesiastical authorities, or their subjects. Assuredly, while sacred pastors devote themselves to the spiritual care of their flock, they also in fact have regard for their social and civil progress and prosperity. According to the nature of their office and as behooves bishops, they collaborate actively with public authorities for this purpose and advocate obedience to just laws and reverence for legitimately constituted authorities. (CD 19)

Christus Dominus then made a statement about the freedom of the church and the end of an age of privileges granted to states:

> This sacred ecumenical synod declares that the right of nominating and appointing bishops belongs properly, peculiarly, and per se exclusively to the competent ecclesiastical authority. Therefore, for the purpose of duly protecting the freedom of the Church and of promoting more conveniently and efficiently the welfare of the faithful, this holy council desires that in future no more rights or privileges of election, nomination, presentation, or designation for the office of bishop be granted to civil authorities. The civil authorities, on the other hand, whose favorable attitude toward the Church the sacred synod gratefully acknowledges and highly appreciates, are most kindly requested voluntarily to renounce the above-mentioned rights and privileges which they presently enjoy by reason of a treaty or custom, after discussing the matter with the Apostolic See. (CD 20)

Even more telling of the status quo perspective of *Christus Dominus* was the passage on the military vicariates (which will play a key role in the church's position in the struggle between democracy and dictatorship in Latin America before and after the council):[24]

> Since, because of the unique conditions of their way of life, the spiritual care of military personnel requires special consideration, there should be established in every nation, if possible, a military vicariate. Both the military vicar and the chaplains should devote themselves unsparingly to this difficult work in complete cooperation with the diocesan bishops. Diocesan bishops should release to the military vicar a

---

[24] See, for example, Loris Zanatta, *Del Estado liberal a la Nación católica. Iglesia y Ejercito en los origenes del peronismo 1930–1943* (Buenos Aires: Universidad Nacional de Quilmes, 1996).

sufficient number of priests who are qualified for this serious work. At the same time they should promote all endeavors which will improve the spiritual welfare of military personnel. (CD 43)

The ambivalence of Vatican II on the issue of the established church was visible also in the *Message to Rulers*, read with the final messages of the council in St. Peter Square on December 8, 1965:

> We proclaim publicly: We do honor to your authority and your sovereignty, we respect your office, we recognize your just laws, we esteem those who make them and those who apply them. But we have a sacrosanct word to speak to you and it is this: Only God is great. God alone is the beginning and the end. God alone is the source of your authority and the foundation of your laws. [. . .] What does this Church ask of you after close to 2,000 years of experiences of all kinds in her relations with you, the powers of the earth? What does the Church ask of you today? She tells you in one of the major documents of this council. She asks of you only liberty, the liberty to believe and to preach her faith, the freedom to love her God and serve Him, the freedom to live and to bring to men her message of life. Do not fear her. She is made after the image of her Master, whose mysterious action does not interfere with your prerogatives but heals everything human of its fatal weakness, transfigures it and fills it with hope, truth and beauty [. . .] We, His humble ministers, allow us to spread everywhere without hindrance the Gospel of peace on which we have meditated during this council. Of it, your peoples will be the first beneficiaries, since the Church forms for you loyal citizens, friends of social peace and progress.[25]

Vatican II strongly reaffirmed the idea of a church of service and not of power, but not without pragmatism and caution. One the one

---

[25] *Message to Rulers*, from Final Messages of Vatican II, December 8, 1965, in Abbott, *The Documents of Vatican II*, 729–30.

hand, Vatican II departs from the ecclesiology of Constantinianism: freedom of conscience and religious liberty, ecumenism, and inter-religious dialogue are major changes from that political-ideological arrangement of church and state in Christendom which needed theological supports that vanished with Vatican II. On the other hand, the council does not proceed to disestablish unilaterally what had been built in centuries (from the church of Constantine in the fourth century to the anti-imperial "Gregorian revolution" of the eleventh century, to the "national" Catholic churches during the rise of the nation states in Europe in the early modern period) in the form of a bilateral agreement between church and the power of the state. Vatican II knew well not only the great diversity of situations for different churches in global Catholicism but also that world politicians, ambassadors, and intelligence agencies were observing it closely.[26]

3. The Established Church in the Post–Vatican II Period and in Pope Francis

The Catholic Church as an institution has been changed only incompletely by the ecclesiology of Vatican II, and some key institutions of the global Catholic Church are still present as legacies of European Christendom. The most famous of these is the financial contribution the Catholic Church receives annually from taxpayers' money thanks to the Concordat (for example, in Italy and Germany). The council's ecclesiology as it was applied during the post-conciliar period resulted in retaining an institutional status quo that cannot be support everywhere today by the real conditions of the Catholic Church, and especially in those areas of world Catholicism that will be the future of Catholicism—the global South. This ecclesiology amounts to a theological break from the system by which the church is supported ideologically and materially by political power, but it is an ecclesiology that assumes a status quo that Vatican II could not and did not have in mind to change overnight—and the biggest

[26] See Alberto Melloni, *L'altra Roma. Politica e S. Sede durante il Concilio Vaticano II (1959–1965)* (Bologna: Il Mulino, 2000).

change came not from theology or from canon law, but from the world outside.

The post–Vatican II reforms did not change the overall system of relations between church and state, and that is true also for those countries in which the Catholic Church is an established church. There were huge cultural changes, what Stephen Schloesser has identified as the biopolitical crisis of Catholicism.[27] After Vatican II there was a loss of political power by those Catholic and Christian-Democratic parties that made Europe immediately after World War II.[28] But these changes did not lead to a revolution in the established church system: no Concordat was denounced or abrogated. There were updates to the Concordats (in 1957 the German Concordat had been declared constitutional; in 1984 Italy and the Holy See signed a new Concordat that updated the previous one), but nobody, if not radical and anticlerical parties on the fringes, had an interest in spending political capital trying to tear down completely the public role of the church in Western Europe, especially before the fall of the Berlin Wall. Those who believed the age of the Concordats ended with the council were wrong, at least for the era of John Paul II.[29]

In the post–1989/91 world, after the fall of Communism, it was not the church that occupied the space vacated by Communism but the free market. During the *second phase of the post–Vatican II period* between 1985 and the 1990s the social and political role

---

[27] See Stephen R. Schloesser, "'Dancing on the Edge of the Volcano': Biopolitics and What Happened after Vatican II," in *From Vatican II to Pope Francis: Charting a Catholic Future*, ed. Paul Crowley (Maryknoll, NY: Orbis Books, 2014), 3–26.

[28] See Wolfram Kaiser, *Christian Democracy and the Origins of European Union* (Cambridge, UK: Cambridge University Press, 2011), 163–90.

[29] The *Enchiridion dei Concordati. Due secoli di storia dei rapporti Chiesa-Stato* (Bologna: EDB, 2003) begins with the Concordat between Pius VII and Napoleon (1801) and concludes with the agreements and Concordats during the pontificate of John Paul II; Romeo Astorri, "La politica concordataria della Santa Sede dopo il Concilio Vaticano II," in *Fede e diplomazia. Le relazioni internazionali della Santa Sede nell'età contemporanea*, ed. Massimo De Leonardis (Milano: Educatt, 2014), 303–20.

of the Catholic Church in European countries changed despite the attempt to slow down the impact of secularization not only through the "new evangelization" but also through the classic diplomatic tools for the strengthening of the public role of the church.[30] The church lost its fight for a European Union founded on the "Christian roots" of the continent, and a decade later the European Union lost its soul unity around the European project.[31] In the quarter century after the end of Communism, John Paul II and then Benedict XVI had to walk a fine line: on the one hand the Catholic Church became the most important global advocate of human rights and religious liberty in the world.[32] On the other hand, the papacy had no intention of giving up the church privileges accrued in the previous century through Vatican diplomacy and a skillful managing of the legacy of the temporal power (for example, as of today in Italy there is still no law on religious freedom).

How did that change with Pope Francis? Francis has never spoken in general terms of the kind of legal and constitutional treatment Catholics should get or look for in a particular country; the legal and political framework of each church is very different and Francis is very aware of that. Francis's ecclesiology favors a Catholic Church free from the protections of the established church in a confessional state, and he spoke openly in favor of a secular state (in Italian, *stato laico*) and against the nostalgia for the confessional state.[33]

---

[30] But see also *La diplomatie de Jean Paul II*, ed. Joël-Benoît D'Onorio (Paris: Cerf, 2000).

[31] See the May 6, 2016, speech Pope Francis gave in the Sala Regia in the Vatican, in accepting the prestigious Charlemagne Prize; http://w2.vatican.va/content /francesco/en/speeches/2016/may/documents/papa-francesco_20160506 _premio-carlo-magno.html.

[32] See Samuel P. Huntington, *The Third Wave: Democratization in the Late Twentieth Century* (Norman: University of Oklahoma Press, 1991).

[33] "States must be secular. Confessional states end badly. That goes against the grain of History. I believe that a version of laicity [English translation for the French *laïcité*] accompanied by a solid law guaranteeing religious freedom offers a framework for going forward. We are all equal as sons (and daughters) of God and with our personal dignity. However, everyone must have

Francis's ecclesiology is based on a practical ecclesiology close to the theology of liberation and its attention to political praxis. Francis comes from Latin American Catholicism that presupposes unity (including mystical unity) between church and people. The prophetic voice of his Catholicism is part of the post–Vatican II, late twentieth-century Christianity that is at the same time an insider part of the system and an outsider critic of it. It is an ambivalence that is also typical of Francis and that he brought to the papacy in a way that differs from a similar ambivalence of the other post–Vatican II popes.

But if Francis is ambivalent, he shares the ambivalence of the council and of *Gaudium et Spes*.[34] He is in no way nostalgic of the past, when church and State were allied. Noteworthy is the fact that in Italy Francis has gone against some of the old features of the established national Catholicism created by the Concordat (which was updated in 1984 but is still in force) between Pius XI and the Fascist regime of Benito Mussolini, and not only by asking forgiveness of the Pentecostal churches persecuted under the Fascists—he is

---

the freedom to externalize his or her own faith. If a Muslim woman wishes to wear a veil, she must be able to do so. Similarly, if a Catholic wishes to wear a cross. People must be free to profess their faith at the heart of their own culture not merely at its margins. The modest critique that I would address to France in this regard is that it exaggerates laicity. This arises from a way of considering religions as sub-cultures rather than as fully-fledged cultures in their own right. I fear that this approach, which is understandable as part of the heritage of the Enlightenment, continues to exist. France needs to take a step forward on this issue in order to accept that openness to transcendence is a right for everyone": Pope Francis, interview with the French Catholic magazine *La Croix*, May 16, 2016, http://www.la-croix.com/Religion/Pape /INTERVIEW-Pope-Francis-2016-05-17-1200760633. (English translation published in *Global Pulse Magazine*, http://www.globalpulsemagazine.com /news/interview-with-pope-francis-by-la-croix/3184).

[34] "It is very easy to slip unconsciously towards positions that may be associated with neo-Constantinianism or, on the contrary, towards positions that may be accused of naïve otherworldliness": Roberto Tucci, "La vie de la communauté politique," in *L'Église dans le monde de ce temps*, ed. Yves Congar and Michel Peuchmaurd (Paris: Cerf, 1967), 2:517.

the first pope to do that.[35] On the plane of more concrete and less historical issues, Francis invited church-owned businesses in Italy (such as the "religious hotels" in Rome) to pay taxes like the other businesses; he started to clean up the Vatican bank, which was one the safe havens created after the Concordat of 1929 by the legal fiction that is the Vatican State; he advocated a more humane policy towards migrants and refugees, knowing that this will make of Italy a state more multicultural, more multi-religious, and sociologically less Catholic.

The second factor is that Francis has a particular way of addressing political issues. The Jesuit Jorge Mario Bergoglio does not shy away from denouncing the injustices of our economic system, but he is very aware of the risks for the pope to be manipulated by politicians (as it happened between popes and Italian politicians until Francis's election). Francis wants to keep politicians at arm's length and he does nothing to hide that. On the other hand, what he is doing is trying to rehabilitate politics.[36] In doing that, he is not advocating a revolutionary change, and certainly not a change in which the public role of the church is less visible and less authoritative. For that matter, Francis's view of the church is not as liberal or radical as many credit him with: it is still a church that demands attention, respect, and a role in the public square. In other words, his radicalism must not be mistaken for a political theology that advocates the radical end of the "established church" where it still exists.

But what is relevant here is his perception of the signs of the times and of his ecclesiology in response to the signs of the times. Which leads us to the third factor: Francis is a radical, social Catholic defending a way of life and a social system that is threatened by what in the encyclical *Laudato Sì* he called "the technocratic

---

[35] See http://w2.vatican.va/content/francesco/en/speeches/2014/july /documents/papa-francesco_20140728_caserta-pastore-traettino.html. About this, see Raffaele Nogaro and Sergio Tanzarella, *Francesco e i pentecostali. L'ecumenismo del poliedro* (Trapani: Il Pozzo di Giacobbe, 2015).

[36] See Diego Fares, "Papa Francesco e la politica," *Civiltà Cattolica* 3976 (February 27, 2016): 373–86.

paradigm."[37] Francis is a progressive Catholic—progressive in the sense of a Catholic with no nostalgia for an idealized past. But there is, to be sure, an antimodern sensibility in him that is typical of Catholic thinkers of the 1930s (the decade he was born), such as Romano Guardini, whom he quotes more than once in *Laudato Sì*.

My contention here is that the reluctance of Catholics rooted in the theology of Vatican II, such as Pope Francis, to do away with the established church is connected to the role the church plays in the world of the "technocratic paradigm." We must ask ourselves if the established church is perhaps one of the few remaining bastions against the destruction of the welfare state, against "turbo capitalism," against the radical individualization of human life, and against neo-imperialism and exceptionalism in the United States of America—a neo-imperialism and exceptionalism in which Constantinianism has survived and survives disestablishment. It is not just about the amount of social work and welfare the church can provide with taxpayers' money allowed by the Concordats; it is not merely about charities and philanthropic initiatives, but also about the work that the government outsourced to the churches a long time ago in some cases and that is now an integral part of the social-economic system.

This fear of the impact of the "technocratic paradigm" is a big factor. A radical withdrawal of the church from the public square would probably mean losing the pulpit that allows the Catholic Church to have a platform and speak in favor and on behalf of those who are excluded from the economic system. In some context, that pulpit that lets the church be present in the public square is funded with privileges that we consider premodern (such as Catholic religion classes in public schools, tax exemptions for charitable initiatives, and so forth), but it is also the last defense against the impact of the "technocratic paradigm."

This reluctance of letting go of that pulpit is not just one of the deep continuities between Francis and his predecessors. It is also one of the transversal issues that mark a clear difference between the

---

[37] Francis, encyclical *Laudato Sì* (May 24, 2015), par. 101ff.

Euro–Latin American Catholicism of Francis and the Catholicism of the Anglo-Saxon world. In the Anglo-Saxon world not only is the very idea of giving taxpayers' money to a church that opposes key elements of the capitalistic system perceived as ridiculous. There is also an ideological issue: in the Anglo-Saxon world political liberalism and theological liberalism are much more aligned and more overlapping than in Europe or anywhere else. This difference between the Euro–Latin American Catholicism of Francis and the Catholicism of the Anglo-Saxon world affects the kind of relationship Catholics have toward the past (including Constantinianism and the established church) and therefore their ideas of "church reform."

As important as the "liberal versus conservative" divide is, the established church dilemma is one of the many examples of the redefinition of the rifts within global Catholicism. But the importance of this is that in Francis there is a genuine ambivalence about the role of the church in the public square: a church that does not want to be politicized, but reclaims its right and duty to be political as it is necessary for a prophetic church. This is not just ambivalence, but a dilemma that is caused by the profound changes in the role of the church in our globalized world.

4. The "Brave New World" and the Established Church

During the first half of the twentieth century and the immediate post–Vatican II period the fight against Constantinianism and the established church was about a Catholic Church that was still (in theory, often less in practice) exclusive in the sense that membership in the Catholic Church defined the legal and social status of all members of the social and political community.

The new prophetic role of the churches in our time should lead us to ask new questions about the old equation between Constantinianism and imperial church on one side and the established church system on the other side. The Catholic Church of today—at least the church of Pope Francis—is much more inclusive both theologically and in practice than the church that signed the Concordat with Mussolini in 1929, with Hitler in 1933, and with Franco in 1953.

We are not in the 1930s, or in the 1950s, and not even at the time of Vatican II. The argument of this chapter is *not* to maintain privileges for the Catholic Church or other churches that still enjoy the special status granted them by Concordats or similar juridical agreements with nation states. Nor it is about advocating new privileges in any way, shape, or form.

In choosing Francis as a name, Jorge Mario Bergoglio was surely aware that the early criticism against the Constantinian church came from those "heretical movements" (to which early Franciscans were close) that saw in the gift of Constantine to the church a dangerous legacy.[38] The poor church that Francis advocates cannot mean going back to the past of Christendom.

What this means is reconsidering the role of the church in the brave new world we live in, and against the backdrop of the macro-crisis of our time.

The constitutional crisis: the doctrine of the church and the state as parallel "perfect societies" has fallen; ironically enough, the state collapsed only a few decades after Catholics accepted its legitimacy.[39] Declining as it is the legitimacy of the established churches, the resilience of church and state nevertheless is a reminder of what I believe is the valuable dualism—between church and state, between *regnum* and *sacerdotium*—a dualism that Ernst-Wolfgang Böckenförde says is essential for a healthy constitutional system.[40]

The ideological crisis: after the end of Marxism, Catholicism might well be the last universalism facing the universalism of the free market, or the divine status of the free market as a god. The church could be one of the last places for the perpetuation of utopia and prophecy in

[38] About this, see Giuseppe Ruggieri, "Prefazione," in Zamagni, *Fine dell'era costantiniana*, 10.

[39] See Paolo Prodi, *Il tramonto della rivoluzione* (Bologna: Il Mulino, 2015), 85.

[40] See Ernst-Wolfgang Böckenförde, *Recht, Staat, Freiheit: Studien zur Rechtsphilosophie, Staatstheorie und Verfassungsgeschichte* (Frankfurt a.M.: Suhrkamp, 2006) and *Kirche und christlicher Glaube in den Herausforderungen der Zeit. Beiträge zur politisch-theologischen Verfassungsgeschichte 1957–2002* (Berlin: LIT, 2007).

front of the death of revolution.[41] The nation state once was claiming total political obedience. The crisis of the nation state in recent years led non-state actors to claim a similar kind of total, blind obedience, in an exchange of roles between religion and politics facing utopia: religion is no longer the advocate of the status quo, politics is no longer the voice of the dreamers.

The cultural crisis:[42] the possible end of the university as the place for independent and creative thinking should remind us that in the Middle Ages the university was the third power between *sacerdotium* and *regnum.*[43] In this sense the role of Catholic colleges and universities could not be greater—granted that they can address the theological crisis that we see in the form of mutual exclusion (if not excommunication) between different theological cultures within Catholicism.

The great political, social, and economic changes in the world during these last fifty years require a new ecclesiological appraisal of the "Constantinian age." The churches today help many human beings survive the deep injustices of the neoliberal system. But the churches also build a substantial, if intangible and immaterial, alternative world-view and they do that also thanks to a vast structure (material and immaterial) that made of the church a partner of the Empire and of the empires of today (whatever we want to call it). But the church also built a counter-empire. Both the imperial and counter-imperial souls of the church were built thanks to the alliance between two suspicious allies, Constantine and the church, and to the way in which antagonistic alliance developed in the centuries afterwards.

To be clear, I have no intention of romanticizing the good old days of the established church. With Vatican II's Declaration on Religious Liberty (*Dignitatis Humanae*), the Catholic Church declared the end of the Constantinian age by giving up the idea of a "Catholic

---

[41] See Terry Eagleton, *Reason, Faith, and Revolution: Reflections on the God Debate* (New Haven, CT: Yale University Press, 2009).

[42] About this, see Terry Eagleton, *Culture* (New Haven, CT: Yale University Press, 2016).

[43] See Prodi, *Università dentro e fuori.*

state." While expressing anguish over secularization, the magisterium of the Catholic Church never reconsidered that fundamental step made by the council and the "status quo ante" narrative, that is, the polemics against Vatican II can do nothing to resuscitate the confessional state.[44] The church has learned a great deal from the modern world about the theological need to acknowledge modern rights (religious liberty above all), and still has to learn something.

I just believe that the changed conditions in our world, and the changed roles between church and states and more exactly between church, the political authority, and non-state actors could lead us to consider what we can let go of in the established church and what is worth retaining, or at least to understand better in its historical and political complexity the role of the Catholic Church today.

Postscript

I wrote the core of this chapter during the week when Pope Francis, patriarch of Constantinople Bartholomew, and archbishop of Athens and all Greece Hieronimus II went to the Greek island of Lesbos to meet the refugees on April 16, 2016.[45]

During that day, when Francis rescued twelve Muslim refugees from that detention camp and took them to Rome on the papal flight, I surprised myself thanking God for the extraterritoriality of the Vatican, the sovereignty of the Vatican State, and the legacy of the temporal power of the pope.

On the one hand, Francis put his pontificate deeply at odds with a century of ideological conversions to Catholicism, from Carl Schmitt in Nazi Germany to Richard John Neuhaus in the United States of the

---

[44] About the survival of a Constantinian age mentality in the magisterial emphasis on "natural law," see Legrand, "Introduction. L'articulation entre annonce de l'Évangile, morale et législations civiles à l'ère post-constantinienne," in *Évangile, moralité et lois civiles. Gospel, Morality, and Civil Law*, 30–32.

[45] See the press conference of Pope Francis during the flight from the island of Lesbos to Rome, April 16, 2016, https://w2.vatican.va/content/francesco/en/speeches/2016/april/documents/papa-francesco_20160416_lesvos-volo-ritorno.html.

"culture wars." On the other hand, at a deeper level, what happened that day on Lesbos says something not just about Pope Francis but about the church in its everyday operations. The refugees on that island and the poor served by the church every day do not know theology, but they know the church. This is true for Christian and non-Christian refugees alike.

In the old continent, Europe, now facing the most serious humanitarian challenge since the end of World War II, they know the church also because of its physical, territorial, and political persistence thanks to the centuries of established Christianity. This is not a case for nostalgia, but for a deeper understanding of the role of the church in the public square today.

Chapter Five

An Interrupted Reception
of *Gaudium et Spes*

The Church and the Modern World
in American Catholicism

Introduction

The opening line of the Pastoral Constitution on the Church in the
Modern World (*Gaudium et Spes*) is challenging today in a world in
which "joy and hope" seem to be in short supply, particularly when
we think about the perception of the role of religion in world affairs
and particularly the relationship between religious identities and
the idea of a shared *civitas*. This is one of those moments when one
remembers that the opening line, given the title *Gaudium et Spes*,
"joys and hopes," was changed from the original, *Luctus et Angor*,
"grief and anxiety."

On the other hand, the reports of the death of Vatican II and
Gaudium et Spes have been greatly exaggerated. *Gaudium et Spes*
has come back in the language of the papal magisterium in a way that
was difficult to predict even for the most optimistic among Catholic
theologians. A big change happened in the church with the election
of Pope Francis, and with it also a change for the role of the pastoral
constitution in the way of thinking and speaking of the church.

It is increasingly clear that *Gaudium et Spes* is one of the great
theological achievements of Vatican II, not only for what it says but
especially for how it says it and how it arrives to say it—that is, for
its theological method.[1] It is not an accident that *Gaudium et Spes* is

---

[1] See Christoph Theobald, *La réception du concile Vatican II*, vol. 1: *Accéder
à la source* (Paris: Cerf, 2009), 695 and 787; Christoph Theobald, *Le Concile*

the document that did not have a preparatory schema in the period before the opening of the council (1960–1962) and that it is the last document approved by a council of learning conciliar fathers for a learning church.[2]

It cannot be denied, however, that *Gaudium et Spes*, especially for the role it plays in Vatican II as a corpus and as an event, needs a new appraisal that is aware of the gap between the church of *Gaudium et Spes* in modernity and in the postmodern world.[3] *Gaudium et Spes* fixes the gaze of the church on a world in flux—a flux that accelerated enormously after the council ended on December 8, 1965.[4] The advent of biopolitics together with the new forms of governmentality,[5] the widening of the horizons of the Catholic Church on the global scene and therefore the discovery of a great complexity and diversity within Catholicism itself, the new relationship between religion and politics after the mid-1970s, especially in our post-9/11 world—these and other elements must be part of the historical-cultural lens through which we read and interpret *Gaudium et Spes* today.[6] The world has changed since 1965, and the church in it has changed as well. The conditions of believing and of belonging have changed to a degree that no single theological, no single ideological

---

Vatican II. Quel avenir? (Paris: Cerf, 2015), 159–80. About this, see the role of *Gaudium et Spes* in the recent debate on Vatican II: Massimo Faggioli, "Vatican II: Bibliographical Survey 2013–2016," *Cristianesimo nella Storia* 37, no. 3 (2016): 235–75

[2] For the history of *Gaudium et Spes*, the standard is still Giovanni Turbanti, *Un concilio per il mondo moderno. La redazione della costituzione pastorale "Gaudium et spes" del Vaticano II* (Bologna: Il Mulino, 2000).

[3] See Terry Eagleton, *The Illusions of Postmodernism* (Oxford: Blackwell, 1996).

[4] See Massimo Faggioli, "Reading the Signs of the Times through a Hermeneutics of Recognition: *Gaudium et Spes* and Its Meaning for a Learning Church," *Horizons* 43, no. 2 (2016): 332–50.

[5] See Michel Foucault, *The Birth of Biopolitics: Lectures at the Collège de France, 1978–1979* (Picador, 2010).

[6] See Stephen R. Schloesser, "'Dancing on the Edge of the Volcano:' Biopolitics and What Happened after Vatican II," in *From Vatican II to Pope Francis: Charting a Catholic Future*, ed. Paul Crowley (Maryknoll, NY: Orbis Books, 2014), 3–26.

school, no single pope can be credited or indicted for such a transformation in the global world and in global Catholicism.[7]

Gaudium et Spes is Vatican II's last word and it addresses in a special way the issue of globalization of Catholicism in the modern world. That is why reflecting on this constitution today is particularly important exactly because of this particular moment in the life of the church and in our lives as citizens. *Gaudium et Spes* calls us also as citizens, because the pastoral constitution has in mind a multifaceted kind of relationship between the church and the modern world: there are elements of a Catholic "political culture" articulated by Vatican II, a culture that conveys the bonds between the advent of social democracy, the Catholic tradition, and fidelity to the Gospel.[8] *Gaudium et Spes* plays an important and unique role in the intra-Catholic debate today, because of the particular role of Vatican II and of *Gaudium et Spes* for Pope Francis on the one hand and, on the other hand, because of the particularly problematic relationship between Pope Francis and the Catholic Church in the United States—what I called Francis's "American problem," one of the hermeneutical keys to understanding his pontificate in global Catholicism.[9]

Taking for granted that there is a particular connection between the way *Gaudium et Spes* was received in the Catholic Church in a particular national context and the social-political posture of the church in a particular nation today, this analysis starts from the hypothesis that there is a gap between the global reception of *Gaudium et Spes* and the reception in the United States, and that it has to do with the particular evolution and involution of the role of American Catholicism in the public square.

---

[7] See Charles Taylor, *A Secular Age* (Cambridge, MA: Belknap Press, 2007); *Church and People: Disjunctions in a Secular Age*, ed. Charles Taylor, Jose Casanova, and George F. McLean (Washington, DC: Council for Research in Values & Philosophy, 2012); Grace Davie, *Religion in Britain since 1945: Believing without Belonging* (Oxford: Wiley-Blackwell, 1994).

[8] See Emile Perreau-Saussine, *Catholicism and Democracy: An Essay in the History of Political Thought* (Princeton, NJ: Princeton University Press, 2012).

[9] See Massimo Faggioli, *Pope Francis: Tradition in Transition* (Mahwah, NJ: Paulist Press, 2015), 61–84.

1. Reception of *Gaudium et Spes* in Post–Vatican II Global Catholicism

A reflection on the reception and interpretation of *Gaudium et Spes* in America today would need to be introduced by a brief overview of the history of the reception of the document—which requires the cautioning that in the existing literature on Vatican II there is no complete study on the global reception of the pastoral constitution in the post–Vatican II period (magisterium, theology, lived praxis of the church, and ecumenical and interreligious reception).[10]

First, the reception of *Gaudium et Spes* is particularly important for the overall reception of Vatican II because on the one hand the pastoral constitution is the flourishing of two seeds planted early in the history of the council: the opening speech of John XXIII, *Gaudet Mater Ecclesia* of October 11, 1962 and the *Message to the World* of October 20, 1962.[11] On the other hand, the pastoral constitution is in a sense an important moment of reception of Vatican II by Vatican II itself.[12] As German-French Jesuit Christoph Theobald has noted, *Gaudium et Spes* finds its final structure only shortly before the beginning of the fourth and final session of the council, in the late spring of 1965. *Gaudium et Spes* is the sign of the growth of Vatican II in understanding a new method of doing theology in the crucial moment in the history of the document between spring and fall 1965.[13] The pastoral constitution is for the council the way of

---

[10] But see Christoph Theobald, *La réception du concile Vatican II. I Accéder à la source* (Paris: Cerf, 2009), 547–654 (chapter "Une brève histoire de la reception de Vatican II").

[11] About the *Message* of October 20, 1962, see Turbanti, *Un concilio per il mondo moderno*, 119–35; *History of Vatican II*, vol. 1, *The Formation of the Council's Identity: First Period and Intersession (October 1962–September 1963)*, ed. Giuseppe Alberigo and Joseph A. Komonchak (Maryknoll, NY: Orbis Books, 1997), 53–54 and 94.

[12] See Hans-Joachim Sander, "Theologischer Kommentar zur Pastoralkonstitution über die Kirche in der Welt von heute," in *Herders Theologischer Kommentar zum Zweiten Vatikanischen Konzil*, ed. Bernd Jochen Hilberath and Peter Hünermann (Freiburg i.B: Herder, 2005), 5:581–886, at 691.

[13] See Theobald, *Le concile Vatican II. Quel avenir?*, 228.

understanding and developing a theological method of the "signs of the times" that had been used by the council *avant la lettre*—before there was a definition for it—and that had been developed and augmented during the council.[14]

Gaudium et Spes is still often regarded as the final, ultimate victory of progressives at Vatican II. But it is worth remembering, today probably more than ever, that the theological method of the "signs of the times" did not meet the enthusiastic approval of the progressive majority at Vatican II.[15] As Bishop McGrath (one of the most important contributors to the drafting of *Gaudium et Spes*) synthesized a few months after the end of Vatican II: "Never before had a council addressed the secular aspect of Christian life in this broad and systematic way. [. . .] The traditionalists looked at the proposal with suspicion and with a humorous disdain [. . .] But also the progressive theologians [who drafted *Lumen Gentium*] rebelled against all that could amount to an empirical consideration of the world. They insisted that the council had to proceed with the accepted theological method."[16]

Second, *Gaudium et Spes* plays a particular role in post–Vatican II papal teachings. Paul VI shapes the focus of the bishops' synods between 1967 and 1974 "in the footsteps of *Gaudium et Spes*."[17] Paul VI rereads Vatican II and *Gaudium et Spes* with the globality of the church and of the corpus of Vatican II clearly in mind, and in this way he seeks to continue John XXIII's principle of pastorality. There is a continuity between Paul VI and John Paul II, but in John Paul II there is also a stronger emphasis on the institutional dimension—Canon Law, the Catechism, and the magisterial role of the

[14] See ibid. Besides Theobald, the most important contributions to the debate on *Gaudium et Spes* have come recently from Carlos Schickendantz (Argentina-Chile) and Hans-Joachim Sander (Germany-Austria).

[15] See Massimo Faggioli, *A Council for the Global Church: Receiving Vatican II in History* (Minneapolis: Fortress, 2015), 121–41.

[16] See Bishop Marcos McGrath, "La genesis de Gaudium et Spes," *Mensaje* 15, no. 153 (October 1966): 495–502, at 496 (translation from Spanish mine).

[17] Theobald, *La réception du concile Vatican II*, 554.

Roman Curia[18]—and special attention to *Gaudium et Spes* par. 22 about "Christ, the new Adam."[19]

The pontificate of Benedict XVI—Joseph Ratzinger, who in 1966 famously called the pastoral constitution "the problem child" (in German: *Sorgenkind*) of Vatican II[20]—presents a different take on the pastoral constitution: for Ratzinger–Benedict XVI *Gaudium et Spes* embodies the need for the church to bring to the world the Light received from God in order to glorify God in the world, and observations on the theological method of *Gaudium et Spes* are absent from his interpretation of the document. In his thought the interpretation of the "signs of the times" remains "largely shaped by a negative view of modern history and modern society, and little affected by the very nuanced approach in the constitution *Gaudium et Spes.*"[21] It is therefore very interesting to see that one of the most important shifts in emphasis between Benedict XVI and his successor concerns Pope Francis's pastoral approach to doctrine, and this revolves around Francis's reception of the pastoral constitution. Pope Francis sees a particular role for the people and a sense of necessary unity between church and people and culture, which makes

[18] See ibid., 590.

[19] See John Paul II, encyclical *Fides et Ratio* (September 14, 1998), par. 12: "Through this Revelation, men and women are offered the ultimate truth about their own life and about the goal of history. As the Constitution *Gaudium et Spes* puts it, 'only in the mystery of the incarnate Word does the mystery of man take on light.' Seen in any other terms, the mystery of personal existence remains an insoluble riddle."

[20] See Carlos Schickendantz, "¿Una transformación metodológica inadvertida? La novedad introducida por *Gaudium et Spes* en los escritos de Joseph Ratzinger," *Teología y Vida* 57, no. 1 (2016): 9–37, esp. 13. About Joseph Ratzinger's approach to *Gaudium et Spes* see his introduction, in the series of his complete works, to the first of the two volumes dedicated to Vatican II: "Vorwort," in *Zur Lehre des Zweiten Vatikanischen Konzils. Formulierung— Vermittlung Deutung*, Joseph Ratzinger Gesammelte Schriften 7, no. 1 (Freiburg i.Br.: Herder, 2012), 5–9, esp. 6–7.

[21] Theobald, *La réception du concile Vatican II*, 653.

Francis an interpreter of *Gaudium et Spes*.[22] In Francis's thought the pastoral constitution plays a role that is very different from that in Benedict XVI's pontificate. *Gaudium et Spes* has been visibly one of the hermeneutical keys in the most crucial passage of Francis's pontificate—the synodal process of 2014–2015 and the post-synodal apostolic exhortation *Amoris Laetitia* on love in the family.

Third, in the shift typical of this pontificate toward a global Catholicism viewed not exclusively from a European point of view, it becomes more and more important to study the reception of Vatican II locally and globally. The history of the reception of *Gaudium et Spes* is particularly relevant from the perspective of a reception divided along the theological fault lines of the post-conciliar theological debate.[23] The split between different ways of interpreting *Gaudium et Spes* is evident if we analyze the different uses of two key passages of the document: paragraph 22 on "Christ the New Adam" and paragraph 36 on "autonomy of earthly affairs." "Liberal" or "progressive" Catholic theologians tend to leave paragraph 22 out and focus on paragraph 36 for their interpretation of *Gaudium et Spes*, while "conservative" theologians tend to do the opposite.[24]

From a global perspective, *Gaudium et Spes* is one, if not the most eminent, of the examples of a "diversified reception" of the council according to the culture of the local church, with significant differences between Europe, North America, and Latin America, if we want to remain in the Euro-Atlantic area. If the history of the drafting of the constitution is famously about the theological and

---

[22] Lucio Gera, *La teología argentina del pueblo*, ed. Virginia R. Azcuy (Santiago de Chile: Ediciones Universidad Alberto Hurtado—Centro Teologico Manuel Larrain, 2015); Carlos Maria Galli, *Dio vive in città. Verso una nuova pastorale urbana* (Vatican City: Libreria Editrice Vaticana, 2014).

[23] See Massimo Faggioli, *Vatican II: The Battle for Meaning* (Mahwah, NJ: Paulist Press, 2012), esp. 66–90.

[24] See Ellen Van Stichel and Yves De Maeseneer, "*Gaudium et Spes*: Impulses of the Spirit for an Age of Globalisation," *Louvain Studies* 39 (2015–2016): 63–79, esp. 69–71.

cultural divide between the French and the Germans,[25] the history of the reception of *Gaudium et Spes* must be framed in much more global terms and in terms that are no longer of "national" theological cultures, even though national theological cultures play a role, as is clear in the case of the Catholic Church in the United States and in the North American context.

2. *Gaudium et Spes* in the Post-Conciliar Context of North America

To understand the relationship between the Catholic Church in the United States and the pastoral constitution *Gaudium et Spes* and the pastoral shift of the church at Vatican II it is necessary to take a look at the wider context, that is, at points of friction between the message of *Gaudium et Spes* and a large geo-cultural area of the world.

A first point of difference between the pastoral constitution and religion in North America is about the *identification between religion and national identity*, which is one of the legacies of the immigrant church and of the persistence of the national and ethnic churches in North America. Both the text and the spirit of *Gaudium et Spes* are ambivalent about the relationship between Christian identity and the duties of political citizenship, also because of the experiences of the ambiguous relationship between Catholics and authoritarian and totalitarian regimes in Europe in the first part of the twentieth century. On the issue of religion and nationalism, Vatican II is distant from what Robert Bellah called "civil religion" as a system of established rituals, symbols, values, norms, and allegiances that build a political allegiance to the nation (see especially GS 75–76 on patriotism and on the relationship between the church and the political community).[26]

---

[25] See Joseph A. Komonchak, "Le valutazioni sulla *Gaudium et Spes*: Chenu, Dossetti, Ratzinger," in *Volti di fine concilio. Studi di storia e teologia sulla conclusione del Vaticano II*, ed. Joseph Doré and Alberto Melloni (Bologna: Il Mulino, 2000), 115–53.

[26] About the idea of "civil religion," see Robert N. Bellah, "Civil Religion in America," *Dædalus, Journal of the American Academy of Arts and Sciences*

Moreover, in *Gaudium et Spes* the move is an opening of the traditional (traditional for European Catholicism) identification between Catholicism and the idea of the nation toward a more cosmopolitan and global articulation of the identity of Catholics in the modern world. It is not just that the thinkers and drafters of *Gaudium et Spes* came from a European context (France and Germany especially) that, after World War II, rejected nationalism and especially religiously inspired nationalism. The difference is also that *Gaudium et Spes* opens to a plural and multicultural world but still in the assumption of a fundamental unity between people, culture, and church in each particular local context: the pastoral constitution acknowledges the modern state and its compatibility with Catholicism but does not develop the theme of pluralism/plurality *within* the modern state. Together with the Declaration on Religious Liberty (*Dignitatis Humanae*), *Gaudium et Spes* makes impossible the criticism against political modernity accepting democracy, constitutionalism, human rights, and so forth. But Vatican II does not deal yet with the postmodern idea and experience of the nation state. The council took place too early to be able to deal with a plurality and pluralism that radically redefine the legitimacy of public power, in a way that is very different from the European truce stipulated between the nineteenth and the early twentieth centuries between the Empire (and its successors) and the churches that resulted in the modern European nations.

The second point of difference is about *the idea of culture*. One of the differences between Catholicism at Vatican II and Catholicism today is that Catholics today experience a high degree of cultural, ethnical, ethical, and political plurality, which, while already part of the Catholic experience worldwide during the council, was not the

---

96, no. 1 (Winter 1967): 1–21. In this sense the fact that a majority of bishops from the United States at Vatican II was *against* the condemnation of nuclear weapons (vote of December 5, 1965) is a case in point about the particularity of the political culture of American Catholicism: see Willem J. Schuijt, "The Fostering of Peace and the Promotion of a Community of Nations," in *Commentary on the Documents of Vatican II*, ed. Herbert Vorgrimler (New York: Herder and Herder, 1969), 5:344–45; John W. O'Malley, *What Happened at Vatican II* (Cambridge, MA: Belknap Press, 2008), 265–66.

experience of the main drafters of *Gaudium et Spes*: this is very relevant for the importance of the idea of "culture" in the constitution (GS 53–62).[27] On the one hand, in *Gaudium et Spes* Catholic theology and magisterium made peace with the relevance of culture for Catholic theology and the development of the tradition (GS 58–59). On the other hand, there is in the constitution a sense of unity between the church and the world, but also a sense of unity of culture within a nation, region, social class, or ethnic group culminating in the unity of the human race (GS 54). *Gaudium et Spes* is a document that precedes the postmodern breaking up of the idea of culture and its new place vis-à-vis the role of the theological tradition.[28]

In the pastoral constitution the prevailing sense of culture is more in the sense of the German *Kultur* and not in the sense of *cultures* (plural). Today the optimistic universality of the idea of culture in *Gaudium et Spes* has become about the protection of an "identity" framed in a much more idiosyncratic way. The theological debate at Vatican II and in *Gaudium et Spes* is about the new balance between nature and grace, but the element of "culture" intervenes out of the possible reach of the pastoral constitution. As Terry Eagleton put it recently, culture has become "a secular version of divine grace."[29] This "culturalization" of the Catholic identity is a development that took place after the end of Vatican II and the debate leading to *Gaudium et Spes*.

The *Kulturkritik* of *Gaudium et Spes* par. 58 ("the Church, sent to all peoples of every time and place, is not bound exclusively and indissolubly to any race or nation, any particular way of life or any customary way of life recent or ancient") is against a "culturalization" of Christianity, which is a belittling of Christianity and of Catholicism as a culture. As Vincent Miller explained recently: "to think of the Church in cultural terms runs the risk of accepting this disciplining

---

[27] See Roberto Tucci, "The Proper Development of Culture," in *Commentary on the Documents of Vatican II*, 246–87.

[28] See Mark A. Smith, *Secular Faith: How Culture Has Trumped Religion in American Politics* (Chicago: University of Chicago Press, 2015).

[29] Terry Eagleton, *Culture* (New Haven, CT: Yale University Press, 2016), 29.

of truth into sectarian niches that fundamentally compromises the Church's catholic mission."[30]

For *Gaudium et Spes*, the culturalist option is for Catholicism not only strategically but also theologically a mistake. The pastoral constitution relativizes the claim of superiority of a culture, rejects the idea of "uncivilized nations," and reframes the relationship between Jesus and culture, the church and cultures. *Gaudium et Spes* also prevents us from presenting Christianity or Catholicism in terms that are cultural yet not theological. What happened after Vatican II—and what happened *to Gaudium et Spes*—is that "the discourse on cultural studies is itself strikingly exclusive,"[31] and this had an impact not only on the world *ad extra*, but also within Catholicism.[32] The biggest shift, however, is from a canonical idea of "culture"—one singular Catholic culture—to a more pluralistic and historical-critical idea of culture*s* in the global church: but in *Gaudium et Spes* it is a shift that assumes a consensus and does not assume the inevitability of the marginalization of the Gospel. The issue of culture is particularly important in order to compare *Gaudium et Spes* and the attitude of the advocates of a splendidly minoritarian Christianity in a surprisingly (for them) hostile world: "an uncritical affirmation of margins and minorities usually goes hand-in-hand with a suspicion of consensuses and majorities. This is because postmodernism is too young to remember a time when mass political movements rocked the state far more vigorously than any margin or minority has proved capable of doing."[33]

This brings up a third point, that is, *the issue of historicity*. In *Gaudium et Spes* the issue of culture is related to a new understanding

---

[30] Vincent J. Miller, "Ecclesiology, Cultural Change, and the Changing Nature of Culture," in *A Church with Open Doors: Catholic Ecclesiology for the Third Millennium*, ed. Richard R. Gaillardetz and Edward P. Hahnenberg (Collegeville, MN: Liturgical Press, 2015), 81.

[31] Eagleton, *Culture*, 34.

[32] About the consequences of this for American Catholic colleges and universities, see Michael J. Byron, "What's Catholic About It?" *America* (February 8, 2016), http://americamagazine.org/issue/whats-catholic-about-it.

[33] Eagleton, *Culture*, 35.

of places and of time, that is, historicity and its relations to dogma (GS 2 and 4). The mutual relationship between dogmatic language and historical awareness is reframed at Vatican II in the sense of a much more serious appreciation of how much dogma owes to history (looking retrospectively) and therefore how much history is important in the process of understanding the dogmatic tradition (looking prospectively, GS 10). The problem is that the historicity of the church is one of the ideas of the council that is received differently depending on the changing "regimes of historicity":[34] not only because the regime of historicity entailing a framework of relationship with the past has become something different between 1965 and 2016, but also because between the European Catholic theology that shaped *Gaudium et Spes* and North American culture today there is a difference in terms of the role of history in the lived spiritual and cultural experience.

The relationship with historicity in the North American context is different from the one in other contexts and from the European context in particular. It is not just the fact of a shorter historical past, but also a different relationship with the future, especially in North American religious culture, where fundamentalism can be seen not only as a specific way of relating to the past, but also as a symptom of the crisis of the future.

This problem of *Gaudium et Spes* and historicity in the North American context is part of the larger shift toward postmodernism, which brings about the crisis of the grand narratives, even of theological narratives. *Gaudium et Spes* has a grand narrative that does *not* correspond with the idea of progress; one of the main inspirators of the text, Marie-Dominique Chenu, OP, was very skeptical about the idea of a "theology of progress." In the pastoral constitution there is no clear "hermeneutics of history,"[35] but there is a deep sense of

---

[34] See François Hartog, *Regimes of Historicity: Presentism and Experiences of Time*, trans. Saskia Brown (New York: Columbia University Press, 2015; original French, 2002).

[35] Giuseppe Ruggieri, "Zeichen der Zeit. Herkunft und Bedeutung einer christlich-hermeneutischen Chiffre der Geschichte," in *Das Zweite Vatikanische*

historicity: "the signs of the times are the constitutive place for the presentation of the faith."[36] *Gaudium et Spes* is part of what in German is called *Vergangenheitsbewältigung*, that is, "coming to terms with the past." It is part of European Catholicism's effort to deal with the tragic past of the previous decades, especially between World War I and World War II, as well as with a Cold War and a possible global nuclear war seen from the European battleground.

3. *Gaudium et Spes* in the United States

The history of the reception of *Gaudium et Spes* in the United States is part of a larger picture of the reception of Vatican II in one of the most important churches in global Catholicism—in a history of the post–Vatican II period for which we have many narratives but not yet an historiographical debate (not to talk about a consensus).

It is clear, however, that the reception of *Gaudium et Spes* cannot be framed in terms of "ecclesiastical history," that is, a history that takes place exclusively within the walls of the institutional church. Everywhere in the world as well as in the United States, the reception of the council is part of a larger social, cultural, and political change that makes Vatican II part of "the Sixties."[37] This is particularly true for a document like *Gaudium et Spes* that embodied the council's aspirations to reach the *ad extra* of the church in a new vocabulary of solidarity, of friendship—a new ecclesiology of the relationship between the church and "the world of this time" (*in mundo huius temporis*).

What is typical of the reception in the North American context are, in my opinion, two things. On the one hand, there is the scarcity of theological commentaries on Vatican II produced in the United

---

Konzil und die Zeichen der Zeit heute, ed. Peter Hünermann (Freiburg i.Br.: Herder, 2006), 61–70, esp. 66. Ruggieri notes the difference between the positions of Marie-Dominique Chenu, Henri de Lubac, Karl Rahner, and Edwaard Schillebeeckx vis-à-vis *Gaudium et Spes*.

[36] Sander, "Theologischer Kommentar zur Pastoralkonstitution," 699.

[37] See Gerd-Rainer Horn, *The Spirit of Vatican II: Western European Progressive Catholicism in the Long Sixties* (New York: Oxford University Press, 2015).

States: one could wonder whether the reception of the council has been more cultural, social, and political than directly theological (systematic and historical)[38] and historiographical.[39] In other words, *Gaudium et Spes* has shaped the development of American Catholic theology after Vatican II with a commitment to Vatican II as a whole, but without an intellectual and academic commitment to the studies of Vatican II as a *corpus* and as an *act*. The lack of studies and commentaries on the pastoral constitution is telling of a reception of Vatican II that since the very beginning was oriented to a situation that most theologians perceived as developing quickly toward a post–Vatican II and postmodern stage.[40]

[38] For example, see the polemics against the idea of a "procedural republic" in J. Brian Benestad, "Doctrinal Perspectives on the Church in the Modern World," in *Vatican II: Renewal within Tradition*, ed. Matthew L. Lamb and Matthew Levering (New York: Oxford University Press, 2008), 147–64.

[39] See Federico M. Requena, "El impacto del Concilio Vaticano II en la historiografía sobre el catolicismo en Estados Unidos," *Anuario de Historia de la Iglesia* 23 (2014): 279–307, esp. 303–4.

[40] See James Hanvey, "The Challenge and Hope of *Gaudium et Spes*," in *The Church in the Modern World: Fifty Years after* Gaudium et Spes, ed. Erin Brigham (Lanham, MD: Lexington Books, 2015), 3–41; John Hittinger, "*Gaudium et Spes* and the Importance of Political Philosophy," *Josephinum* 20, no. 2 (Summer/Fall 2013): 279–306; James F. Keenan, "Vatican II and Theological Ethics," *Theological Studies* 74 (March 2013): 162–90; Terence Kennedy, "Bernard Häring and Domenico Capone's Contribution to Vatican II," *Studia Moralia* 51, no. 2 (2013): 419–42; William McDonough, "*Gaudium et Spes* on the Gospel as '*lux et vires*' for Our Lives: The '*divine condenscensio*' and Catholic Morality," *Heythrop Journal* 2015 (published online October 30, 2015). See also Michael G. Lawler et al., eds., *The Church in the Modern World:* Gaudium et Spes *Then and Now* (Collegeville, MN: Liturgical Press, 2014), and in particular Vincent Miller, "Ecclesiology, Cultural Change, and the Changing Nature of Culture," in *A Church with Open Doors*, 64–84. These important recent articles cannot hide the fact that American Catholic theological academia has not produced a multivolume commentary or dictionary or systematic series of studies on Vatican II similar to the ones published, for example, in France, Germany, Italy, Spain, Chile, and Brazil. Forthcoming is also a Korean translation of the *Herders Theologischer Kommentar zum Zweiten Vatikanischen Konzil*, ed. Bernd Jochen Hilberath and Peter Hünermann, 5 vols. (Freiburg i.B: Herder, 2004–2005).

On the other hand, there is the divisiveness of the reception of Vatican II, probably more at the level of academic theology than at the level of the people of God (and a divisiveness about the interpretation of Vatican II that is more profound in the United States than anywhere else). This is a phenomenon that remains to be investigated, especially for the relation between this divisiveness and lack of a tradition or school of Vatican II studies in the United States.

All that said, it is undeniable that Vatican II and *Gaudium et Spes* have been received in the church in the United States, especially in the first twenty years after the council.[41] The period between the full participation of American Catholicism in the civil rights movements in the mid-1960s and the letters of the US bishops on nuclear war and on economic justice see an abundant use of the pastoral constitution. *The Challenge of Peace: God's Promise and Our Response* (May 3, 1983) and *Economic Justice for All* (November 1986) represent the highest moment in the reception of Vatican II in the teaching of the US bishops in response to the urgent issues of their time.[42] *Gaudium et Spes* plays a key role in these documents, together with the other documents of Vatican II.

But it is a reception that changes after the mid-1980s, when the pontificate of John Paul II and the influence of Joseph Ratzinger on the pontificate shape the beginning of a different phase in the role of the pastoral constitution in the church. This is part of a complex relationship between two church leaders with different conciliar experiences (John Paul II as a conciliar father and one engaged in the commission for the drafting of *Gaudium et Spes*;[43] Ratzinger

---

[41] For a comparison between the United States and Germany, see *Zeiten der pastoralen Wende? Studien zur Rezeption des Zweiten Vatikanums—Deutschland und die USA im Vergleich*, ed. Andreas Henkelmann and Graciela Sonntag (Münster: Aschendorff, 2015).

[42] See David Hollenbach, "'Economic Justice for All' Twenty Years Later," *Journal of Catholic Social Thought* 5, no. 2 (2008): 315–21.

[43] See, for example, George Weigel, *Witness to Hope: The Biography of Pope John Paul II* (1999; New York: HarperCollins, 2001), 166–69; Gabriel Richi Alberti, *Karol Wojtyla: un estilo conciliar. Las intervenciones de K. Wojtyla en el Concilio Vaticano II* (Madrid: Publicaciones San Dámaso, 2010); Karol Wojtyla,

as a *peritus*) and with different takes on the constitution (if one remembers the writings on the pastoral constitution by the young German theologian in the early 1970s).[44]

The John Paul II–Benedict XVI imprint in the North American context redraws the ecclesial and theological map. Its trajectory leads in the early 2000s to the pre-electoral document of the USCCB *Faithful Citizenship*, approved in 2007 and updated in 2011 (and deliberately not updated in 2015), that would require a separate analysis for its relationship with Vatican II.

4. *Gaudium et Spes* and the Polarization of American Catholicism

The fact that Vatican II is more captive of the ideological "narratives" than of the historiographical and theological debate is part of the larger North American context and not only of Catholicism in the United States.[45] However, there are also specific issues of American Catholicism that have a particular influence on the reception of *Gaudium et Spes*. Here I wish to offer a contribution not just as a church historian but also as a European scholar who moved to the United States a few years ago.[46]

Quelle der Erneuerung. Studie zur Verwirklichung des Zweiten Vatikanischen Konzils (Freiburg i.Br.: Herder, 1981; original Polish, 1971).

[44] See Joseph Ratzinger, "A Review of the Post-Conciliar Era," in *Principles of Catholic Theology* (San Francisco: Ignatius Press, 1987), 367–93. About *Gaudium et Spes* in the context of the immediate post–Vatican II period see Faggioli, *A Council for the Global Church*, 121–41.

[45] See Massimo Faggioli, "Vatican II: The History and The 'Narratives,'" *Theological Studies* 73, no. 4 (December 2012): 749–67.

[46] A few observations about *Gaudium et Spes* and American politics from the Sixties to the USCCB document *Faithful Citizenship* (2007) can be found in Thomas Massaro, "The Role of Conscience in Catholic Participation in Politics since Vatican II," in Brigham, *The Church in the Modern World*, esp. 74–77.

4.1. Gaudium et Spes *and Competitive American Church Politics*

First of all there is an issue of contested reception of *Gaudium et Spes* and of Vatican II in general in the larger social-political context of the United States in these last five decades.

One factor that plays into a particular reception of the pastoral constitution is the reception of a particular pontificate in a particular area of the global church. On the one hand it is clear that the impact of John Paul II and Benedict XVI on American Catholicism is much greater than the impact of Paul VI (whose memory in the United States, unlike in Latin America or even Europe, is largely associated with the teaching on contraception in *Humanae Vitae*) and of Francis (who, since the beginning of his pontificate, faced significant opposition from US Catholicism). On the other hand, the church and the idea of Catholic tradition have been redefined for American Catholics through the pontificates of John Paul II and Benedict XVI (and by the bishops they appointed) in a period that coincides with a time of political realignment and of a new role of Catholics in American politics.[47]

In the United States the apostolic delegate Jean Jadot[48] had made a significant contribution to the formation of the US bishops responsible for the pastoral letters of the USCCB on *The Challenge of Peace* (1983) and on *Economic Justice for All* (1986). But most of all, the USCCB was responsible for managing reform after the Second Vatican Council so that, in the words of Thomas J. Reese, "the American church did not experience a schism [and the bishops] have been very successful adapting episcopal conference structures to the American political and cultural context."[49] On the other hand,

---

[47] About this, see Massimo Faggioli, "What Happened to Vatican II? Italian and US Catholicism in the 1970s and 1980s," in *"Theologia semper iuvenescit". Études sur la réception de Vatican II offertes à Gilles Routhier*, ed. Michael Quisinsky, Karim Schelkens, and François-Xavier Amherdt (Fribourg: Academic Press Fribourg, 2013), 153–79.

[48] Jean Jadot, apostolic delegate in the United States between 1973 and 1980, was replaced by Pio Laghi, apostolic delegate between 1980 and 1990.

[49] See Thomas J. Reese, *A Flock of Shepherds: The National Conference of Catholic Bishops* (Kansas City, MO: Sheed & Ward, 1992), 304–5.

in the United States the "Jadot bishops" were soon replaced, starting in the 1980s, by a new cohort of bishops more carefully chosen on the basis of their doctrinal loyalty to Paul VI's *Humanae Vitae* and John Paul II's magisterium on moral issues.

In the United States John Paul II's pontificate seemed to have accompanied a process that, according to Peter Steinfels, was already underway at the moment of his election: "Beyond noting the differences between Paul VI's and John Paul II's papacies, the prevailing stories of the Council and its aftermath unfortunately differentiate very little between distinct stages. In the United States, the period of greatest turmoil was ending by the late 1970s [. . .] Consolidation in the United States was already under way when John Paul II's own agenda for consolidation began to kick in."[50] The political-religious revival (and the new "religious right") that started with the Carter presidency in 1976 seemed to be a factor totally lacking in other countries, and this meant a new position for US Catholics vis-à-vis culture and politics, and therefore a diminution in the importance of the value of dialogue so evident in *Gaudium et Spes*.

In other words, in the shift inaugurated by John Paul II there was also a particular shift for the reception, or lack of reception, of Vatican II, and the position of *Gaudium et Spes* in the Catholic Church in the United States is part of this. The issue for the pastoral constitution and the *ad extra* dimension of the American Catholic Church is that once again here the experience of a two-party, competitive (and nonconsensual) political system that is so strong in America has spilled over into the culture of Catholics in the United States, and this becomes visible especially in times of a change of pontificate.[51] *Gaudium et Spes* inaugurated a new era in the ecclesiology of the relationship between the church and the modern world, but it did that by reframing the previous Catholic social teaching in a way that is impossible to understand simply in terms of "continuity"

[50] Peter Steinfels, *A People Adrift: The Crisis of the Roman Catholic Church in America* (New York: Simon & Schuster, 2003), 38–39.
[51] See Faggioli, *A Council for the Global Church*, 307–27.

as opposed to "discontinuity" and vice versa.[52] It is worth noting that one of the reasons the USCCB in 2015 could not agree on the need to revise the pre-electoral document *Faithful Citizenship* was exactly a mistaken idea of continuity in the tradition.[53]

4.2. New *Catholic Americanism versus* Gaudium et Spes

There is a second political issue related to substantial characteristics of American political culture that are typical of a fractured reception of *Gaudium et Spes*.

The pastoral constitution is the most important document that makes possible the transition of Catholicism from its traditional European cultural embedding to a truly global Catholicism: culturally diverse and plural. For Catholics this entails a new articulation of the relationship between Catholic identity and national identity in the sense of a much more cosmopolitan universality of Catholicism—a Catholicism that is less *universalist* (in Latin: *universalis*), less anxious about imposing a unified model, and more *universal*, confident in the existence of a global common ground within a very diverse Catholic Church (in Latin, *universa*). In this sense, the equation between Catholicism and Italian culture, or European culture, or Western civilization is over. Any equation between Catholicism and a particular national or regional or ethnic culture is not possible anymore after *Gaudium et Spes*. This is part of the American problem in Francis's Catholicism: the end of what I would call the "American Catholic equation" which is at work on both sides of the aisle in polarized American Catholicism: what is good for American Catholicism is good for both the United States of America *and* for Catholicism. In other

---

[52] A most nuanced interpretation of the famous speech of Benedict XVI of December 22, 2005, on the hermeneutics of Vatican II is in Joseph A. Komonchak, "Benedict XVI and the Interpretation of Vatican II," *Cristianesimo nella Storia* 28, no. 2 (2007): 323–37.

[53] About the USCCB annual meeting of November 2015, see Tom Roberts, "At USCCB Meeting, Bishops Slow to Adopt Pope's Vision," *National Catholic Reporter* (December 1, 2015), http://ncronline.org/news/vatican/parsing -priorities-and-plans-meeting-bishops-slow-adopt-popes-vision.

words, what emerges after the 1980s is *a new Catholic Americanism* different from the one condemned by Leo XIII in 1899, especially considering that a liberal-progressive Catholic Americanism exists side-by-side with and yet opposed to a traditionalist-conservative Catholic Americanism.[54]

The issue, however, is not just in the "American equation" in itself, but also with what this Americanism became within the turn of American Catholicism in the second half of the post–Vatican II period, that is, with what the hierarchical leadership of American Catholicism became after the mid-1980s.

A first instance of a particular way of receiving *Gaudium et Spes* concerns the most divisive moral issues in America today. More than any other Catholic Church in the world, the hierarchy of the American Catholic Church became overwhelmed by the challenge of biopolitics (the "life issues" in particular) much more than by the perception of a rapidly collapsing social fabric being held together by the welfare state and by a more just socioeconomic system. The pastoral letter *Economic Justice for All* of 1986 was the last time the US bishops spoke boldly about the systemic injustices of our economy; it is known that in 2012 the US bishops were unable to agree on a draft of a new letter on the social and economic justice (and to date the bishops' conference has been silent on the issue).[55]

Over the last few years the American episcopate has been showing a particularly "Americanist" reception of the teaching of Vatican II.[56] The wider moral and epistemological picture drawn by *Gaudium*

---

[54] The development of Catholic moral and political theology during these last fifty years in the United States would require a much more detailed analysis.

[55] See John Gehring, "Two Steps Back," *Commonweal* (June 3, 2016): 19–22. Among the US bishops speaking on these issues, see Robert W. McElroy, "A Church for the Poor," *America* (October 21, 2013), and "The Greatness of a Nation," *America* (February 15, 2016).

[56] An eminent example of this was the USCCB campaign about religious liberty, whose foundational document was based much more on a legal-constitutional argument (the American Constitution) than a theological one (the declaration *Dignitatis Humanae* and the constitution *Gaudium et Spes*): see USCCB, *Our First, Most Cherished Liberty: A Statement on Religious Liberty* (March 2012) http://www

et Spes for the church in the modern world seemed lost on most bishops in the United States. It is also an issue of the reception of the council in a larger religious context of the United States in which Catholicism became slowly a nationally relevant church building on a previous layer of Protestant Calvinism and, within Catholicism, with the legacy of a political Augustinianism that gives Christianity authority over the State.

Hierarchical Catholicism in the United States does not always seem comfortable with *Gaudium et Spes* because it is a document that is not about power and authority but about salvation and liber-ation.[57] The assonance between *Gaudium et Spes* and Pope Francis is not accidental. There is surely a problem of conflating faith with conservative ideology, but it is also more generally a problem of reception of the ecclesiology of Vatican II.

A second instance of "Americanist" nonreception of Vatican II and *Gaudium et Spes* in particular was the reception of John Paul II's teaching on social justice and the modern economy, which in the United States was subject to a particularly effective interpretation as a papal endorsement of the neoliberal capitalist system. The oc-casion was John Paul II's encyclical *Centesimus Annus* (1991): the mainstream interpretations of it in the center of global capitalism were captive of a particular ideological tradition, and this gave rise to the neo-conservative stream within American Catholicism.[58]

A third instance of an "Americanist" non-reception of the global rephrasing of the moral teaching of *Gaudium et Spes* during this

---

.usccb.org/issues-and-action/religious-liberty/our-first-most-cherished-liberty
.cfm.

[57] See Sander, *Kommentar*, 693.

[58] See Anthony Annett, "The Fall of the House of Neuhaus," *dotCom-monweal*, March 21, 2016, https://www.commonwealmagazine.org/blog /fall-house-neuhaus. Cardinal Peter Turkson (president of the Pontifical Council for Justice and Peace) acknowledged the ideological manipulations *Centesimus Annus* was subject to in a lecture at a conference hosted by the Catholic University of America's School of Business and Economics and the Napa Institute in March 2016; http://en.radiovaticana.va/news/2016/03/17 /card_turkson_lectures_on_laudato_si_in_business/1216276.

last decade was about the United States and the new situation of international relations, and in particular war and peace in a post-9/11 world: it is the moral failure of large sectors of the American Catholic hierarchy and Catholic academia to address the hypocrisies of neo-militarism within American military culture.[59]

On the other hand, the liberal-progressive side of American Catholicism is not innocent of a dismissal of *Gaudium et Spes*: the emphasis on identity politics even within the church can be interpreted as the forgetting of the fundamental idea of *unity* that is at the basis on Vatican II as well as of the pastoral constitution. It is undeniable that the idea of "common good" (*bonum commune*: GS 26, 30, 42, 43, 59–60, 65, 67–68, 71, 73–75, 78, 84) at Vatican II was part of the assumption of a given cultural, political, social, and theological *status quo* that was presumed stable: it was before racial, gender, and sexual diversity arrived on the stage of the Catholic Church. But the postmodern dismissal of the value of unity and the ideological emphasis on diversity and plurality on the one side and the farewell to the common good by communitarian thinkers on the other side[60] have contributed to give us "its anthropological narrative, in today's mass narcissism, [that] does not create democracy out of differences, but rather out of obsessive micro-conflict of identity."[61]

It is evident how much these three "Americanist" issues are part of the picture of the complex relationship between the pontificate of Pope Francis and American Catholicism. But, overall, there is a larger issue of *Gaudium et Spes* replacing the pre–Vatican II binomium (geographical *particularity* of the places of pastoral care, connected with an assumed *universalism* of a culturally Western, idiosyncratic representation of the Gospel) with a more plural "topology" of the

---

[59] I can refer here to the works of Andrew J. Bacevich, especially *The New American Militarism: How Americans Are Seduced by War* (New York: Oxford University Press, 2005).

[60] About Alasdair MacIntyre's *After Virtue* and the idea of common good, see David Hollenbach, "The Common Good Revisited," *Theological Studies* 50 (1989): 70–94, esp. 77–79.

[61] Pierangelo Sequeri, *L'amore della ragione. Variazioni sinfoniche su un tema di Benedetto XVI* (Bologna: EDB, 2012), 90.

church teaching (multiculturalism of the representation of the gospel in a globalized church). It is the passage from a church based on "identity" to a church based on "where it stands" (in German: from *Wer-Identität* to *Wo-Frage*).[62]

4.3. Gaudium et Spes *and Augustinianism in American Catholic Ecclesiology*

The particular kind of reception of *Gaudium et Spes* in the United States must be seen in the context of post–Vatican II ecclesiology in this theological and ecclesial context. Ecclesiological reflection in the United States is lively and is engaged in the reception of Vatican II.[63] But the fragmentation of American Catholicism had consequences for the ecclesiological reception of *Gaudium et Spes*.[64] The separation between the ecclesiological reflection in American Catholic academia and the ecclesiology taught and practiced during priestly formation in seminaries plays a key role. We must go back to the times of Avery Dulles's *Models of the Church* for an ecclesiologist able to bridge these two worlds that now seem completely separated, with serious consequences for both the life of the church and Catholic theology.[65]

The relations between ecclesiology and the emphasis (typical of Catholicism in the United States) on Catholic social doctrine are part of the picture. This emphasis stresses a continuity between Catholic social doctrine today and its beginning in the modern period with

[62] See Sander, *Kommentar*, 696–98.

[63] See, for example, the activity of the "Vatican II Studies Group" and "Ecclesiological Investigations Group" at the American Academy of Religion; the annual conferences of the Ecclesiological Investigations International Research Network, http://ei-research.net/. A *status quaestionis* for ecclesiology today is the Festschrift for Thomas O'Meara, *A Church with Open Doors: Catholic Ecclesiology for the Third Millennium*, ed. Richard R. Gaillardetz and Edward P. Hahnenberg (Collegeville, MN: Liturgical Press, 2015).

[64] About the early rift in the different interpretations of *Gaudium et Spes*, see Joseph A. Komonchak, "Augustine, Aquinas, or the Gospel *sine glossa?*," in *Unfinished Journey: The Church 40 Years after Vatican II; Essays for John Wilkins*, ed. Austin Ivereigh (New York and London: Continuum, 2005), 102–18.

[65] See Avery Dulles, *Models of the Church* (New York: Image Books, 1974).

Leo XIII's *Rerum Novarum*, but without considering that in the nineteenth-century social teaching of the church "the non-exclusion of the social realm had no consequence on the systematic level of presentation of the faith."[66] A similar attempt to highlight Vatican II's continuity with the past, underestimating the importance of change in teaching, emphasizes the link between Trent, eighteenth-century Catholicism, and twentieth-century theology.[67]

There are clear discontinuities between Vatican II, *Gaudium et Spes*, and the previous period. One novelty of *Gaudium et Spes* is the inclusion of the social realm not as an issue *ad extra*, but as one with ecclesiological consequences within the Catholic Church—and this is something with which many in the Catholic hierarchy in the United States still struggle. The pastoral dimension of the council's teaching is framed in *Gaudium et Spes* through the theological assumption of the history of humankind and of the world in which *Gaudium et Spes* operates: there is a new relevance for a theology of the world *ad extra*, including the secular, that is not part of a shared theological culture in the United States.

The place of "the secular" in *Gaudium et Spes* is one of the problems for its reception in this ecclesial and ecclesiological context, in which the relations between religion and politics in the United States are substantially different from the relations between religion and politics in the culture of those who drafted this pastoral constitution. Particularly different between the circumstances of *Gaudium et Spes* and American Catholic ecclesiology is that "the role of the state is at center of the focus" of chapter 4 (par. 73–76) of the constitution.[68] The section of *Gaudium et Spes* on politics is centered around the issue of power in a "church and State" picture, where the church represents in society and in the public square a particular voice vis-à-vis the power holders in the state: in the pastoral constitution and

[66] Sander, *Kommentar*, 694.

[67] An example is Ulrich L. Lehner, *On the Road to Vatican II: German Catholic Enlightenment and Reform of the Church* (Minneapolis: Fortress Press, 2016), 2–3.

[68] See Sander, *Kommentar*, 797–98.

in Vatican II there is no sacralization of the state (something that is more compatible with the idea of a "civil religion" in America), but nor is there a view of the political and of the secular state as idolatry.[69] Here the conflation between ecclesiology and politics is typical of the political ecclesiology of *Gaudium et Spes* no less than of the radical critics of this aspect of the theology of Vatican II: there is a set of political ideas on both sides.[70]

In other words, there is clearly a transatlantic "God gap" between America and Europe.[71] But there is also a transatlantic "City of God gap" between America and the political culture of Vatican II.[72] The Augustinianism of radical neo-orthodox theologians derives from an incompatibility with the council's definitively post-Augustinian and post-Christendom political ecclesiology: "Vatican II, which quotes abundantly Augustine, managed to liberate the Church from 'political Augustinianism' thanks to *Gaudium et Spes* and *Dignitatis Humanae* on religious liberty. [. . .] The revolution of Thomas Aquinas

---

[69] The contribution of the political culture of theologians and thinkers close to the Christian-Democratic parties in post–World War II Europe is fundamental to the Catholic internationalism and an idea of the state in *Gaudium et Spes*: see Wolfram Kaiser, *Christian Democracy and the Origins of European Union* (Cambridge, UK: Cambridge University Press, 2011); Giuseppe Dossetti, *Non abbiate paura dello Stato! Funzioni e ordinamento dello Stato moderno!*, ed. Enzo Balboni (Milan: Vita e Pensiero, 2014; new edition of a text delivered by Dossetti in 1951); *Christian Democrat Internationalism: Its Action in Europe and Worldwide from Post–World War II until the 1990s*, ed. Jean-Dominique Durand, 3 vols. (Brussels: Peter Lang, 2013–2014).

[70] About this, see Hans Joachim Sander, "Das Aggiornamento des Zweiten Vatikanischen Konzils. Ein radikales Ereignis wider theologische und politische Radikalismen," in *Radikalität. Religiöse, politische und künstlerische Radikalismen in Geschichte und Gegenwart*, vol. 2, *Frühe Neuzeit und Moderne*, ed. Lena-Simone Günther, Saskia Hertlein, Bea Klüsener, and Markus Raasch (Würzburg: Könighausen & Neumann, 2013), 79–102.

[71] See Thomas Albert Howard, *God and the Atlantic: America, Europe, and the Religious Divide* (New York: Oxford University Press, 2011).

[72] One recent example is Hittinger, Gaudium et Spes *and the Importance of Political Philosophy*, esp. 302–4.

and Albert the Great had already produced theologically a decisive break in the system of political Augustinianism."[73]

In the theology of Vatican II the power of the state is also the welfare state at the service of human development, the constitutional self-restraint of political power, and the protection of fundamental human rights in the context of the overcoming of the tragic experiences of the first half of the twentieth century.[74] Christian and Catholic radicalism in the United States, however, sees in the power of the state chiefly the paradigm of violence and the danger of the sacralization and idolization of the nation and the state.[75]

On the other hand, American Catholic ecclesiology has been very receptive—even more so than other contexts—to another aspect of this ambivalence of Vatican II, that is, the prophetic stance based on a new understanding of the role of conscience (GS 16) connected with a new understanding of religious liberty in *Dignitatis Humanae*. It is true that the prophetic stance of Dorothy Day, the *Catholic Worker*, and the like predate the council by at least three decades and is followed by an American Catholic radicalism (for example, the Berrigan brothers) that has few or no parallels in Europe.

But a radical dismissal of the council's political ecclesiology as compromised with the legacy of the "Constantinian age" forgets that the new Catholic social and political activism in the 1960s was made possible worldwide thanks to the theology of the council as well.[76]

---

[73] Congar, "Église et monde dans la perspective de Vatican II," 31.

[74] See Roberto Tucci, "La vie de la communauté politique," in *L'Église dans le monde de ce temps*, ed. Yves Congar and Michel Peuchmaurd (Paris: Cerf, 1967), 2:517–70.

[75] For a nuanced analysis of Augustine's *City of God*, see David Hollenbach, "The Common Good Revisited," *Theological Studies* 50 (1989): 70–94, esp. 79–85. For an important contribution on the relationship between church and state in which the autonomy of the secular does not presuppose a domain closed off from the divine order, see Brian Trainor, *Christ, Society and the State* (Adelaide: ATF, 2012).

[76] Political scientist Samuel Huntington (1927–2008) pointed out that the process of democratization in the twentieth century is likely to have more to do with the Second Vatican Council than with the spread of the free market in

It is after Vatican II that in a truly global Catholicism it becomes not only theologically clear, but also part of the lived experience of the church, that a prophetic church is essentially political, that the prophets are political, and that the prophet's discourse is essentially political speech and the prophet's horizon is temporal and immanent—qualities that become part of the horizon of the church with *Gaudium et Spes*. Yves Congar saw the pastorality of *Gaudium et Spes* as a rupture with political Augustinianism and its subordination of the temporal order to the supernatural:

> The temporal order has become historic, cosmic, social, centered on a human being conscious of its power of domination and transformation of things and of itself. This is the temporal order or the world that Vatican II looked at. The council recognizes the temporal order its own value, not reducible to its role for the attainment of the supernatural—although it is existentially ordered to the supernatural.[77]

5. America and "the Joys and the Hopes," Fifty Years After

This assessment of the legacy of *Gaudium et Spes* in the United States fifty years after the end of Vatican II started with a look at the global reception of the pastoral constitution, then focused on the role of this particular text in the post-conciliar context in North America, and finally tried to develop an initial analysis of the relationship between *Gaudium et Spes*, American Catholicism today, and American church politics, in the background of what I would call "new Catholic Americanism" and the legacy of political Augustinianism.

---

the vast world beyond the Western European and North American sphere: see Samuel P. Huntington, *The Third Wave: Democratization in the Late Twentieth Century* (Norman: University of Oklahoma Press, 1991).

[77] Yves Congar, "Église et monde dans la perspective de Vatican II," in *L'Église dans le monde de ce temps*, 3:15–41, at 30.

This is a preliminary exploration of a field that will require real research, leading possibly to a history of the political cultures of American Catholics in the post–Vatican II period. Therefore there are no conclusions that precede such research.

There are, however, two hypotheses for the development of this future research that can conclude this brief chapter.

A first hypothesis is that there is a particular connection between the way *Gaudium et Spes* was received in the Catholic Church and the social-political context of that church. *Gaudium et Spes* elaborates on the new opening to the world in a cultural context in which the relations between the church and modern culture change after Vatican II more than they had changed in Europe, for example; the European context was the background of the changes described by Vatican II in the pastoral constitution. Because of the delayed secularization of American culture and politics, the changes happening in the role of the church and religion in the United States, especially in the relations between religion and politics, seems to be originating from that conciliar text which is accused of having somehow "imported" into the United States a culturally and sociologically weakened European Catholicism. This is at the heart of the divided reception of Vatican II and of *Gaudium et Spes* in particular.

The second hypothesis has to do with the role of theological reflection in a church like the Catholic Church in the United States, which is, in its own way, a church of *Gaudium et Spes*. From a mere bibliographical point of view, it is worth mentioning here that the reception of *Gaudium et Spes* in the United States took place *without* a substantial investment from the Catholic academia in the theological meaning of it for the intellectual, spiritual, and cultural tradition of American Catholicism. The weakness of the theological reflection on the history and theology of *Gaudium et Spes* left that ecclesiological shift at the mercy of a political-theological spin that grew louder as the church became chronologically more distant from the event of Vatican II. In this sense, it is impossible to overestimate the impact, especially in the United States, of John O'Malley's *What Happened at Vatican II* in order to recapture the meaning of the whole council and also of *Gaudium et Spes*: "in a world increasingly wracked with discord, hatred, war, and threats of war, the result was a message that was counter-cultural while at the same time responsive to the deepest human yearnings. Peace on earth. Good will to men."[78]

The reception of *Gaudium et Spes* is in great part the symbol of the divided reception of the council and especially of its ecclesiology in America. A series of analyses of the role of *Gaudium et Spes* in the United States will be key also to understanding the reception of Pope Francis in comparison with the roles of John Paul II and Benedict XVI, and ultimately to position this church more accurately on the map of a Catholic Church made global thanks to *Gaudium et Spes* as well.

[78] O'Malley, *What Happened at Vatican II*, 311.

Chapter Six

Ecclesiology of Mercy

A Vision for the Church in the Twenty-First Century

Offering a vision for the church in the twenty-first century is part of the task of the theologian reflecting on "the joys and the hopes" of the followers of Christ in this particular time. If not grounded in a dynamic understanding of the tradition, this vision can easily become an exercise in futurology or in traditionalism. Any ecclesiological reflection on the future path of the church cannot avoid becoming aware of the recent past and of the present situation of the church. Catholicism is not exempt from the obsession with "presentism," the illusion of being able to deal with issues in the Catholic Church based on a vision that is short-sighted toward both the future and the past.

Therefore any ecclesiological vision must be preceded by a brief analysis of the state of the Catholic Church today. My particular analysis will proceed from the point of view of the public role of the church before approaching Pope Francis's contribution to our ecclesial consciousness, and finally exploring a few ideas about a vision for the future church based on Francis's emphasis on mercy.

1. Catholicism and the Public Square in the Age of Francis

If we reflect on the importance of the Jesuits' call to the frontier, it is not a coincidence that the resignification of the boundaries of the church in an inclusive way is taking place during the pontificate of a Jesuit pope. But this redrawing of the boundaries is part of a longer process. Just as the Second Vatican Council redefined the boundaries of the church with an ecclesiology very aware of the *ad extra*

123

dimension of Catholicism, so, too, the post-conciliar period has seen a particular osmosis between the intra-Catholic (the perception of the state of the church) and the *ad extra* (the church and the world).

In a sense, the classical distinction between the *ad intra* and *ad extra*—a key idea for the ecclesiology of Vatican II—is now much less apt to describe the church and its mission today. The boundaries between the *ad intra* and *ad extra* have become more porous: we live in a much more diverse religious landscape coexisting with different religious traditions, different cultural versions of the same religious tradition, different versions of atheism and secular worldviews, in societies in which individuals have overlapping, mutually nonexclusive identities and religious worldviews.

This porousness may be one of the things that Karl Rahner meant in his famous dictum: "The Christian of the future will be a mystic or will not exist at all."[1] It is interesting to note that in the first part of that famous essay, Rahner connected Christian spirituality and the changing position of the church in the public square: "The Church's spirituality in the future—for the Church must always have a spirituality—will also have a sociological, political dimension facing on to the world, bearing a responsibility for this merely apparently secular world; and it may be said at once that this very dimension—which also pertains to spirituality as such—will in the future presumably be more clearly possessed and filled up by the latter."[2]

The different interpretations within Catholicism of what Rahner called "responsibility for this merely apparently secular world" are part of the hermeneutical question of Vatican II, which is centered primarily not on dogmatic issues or on the liturgy, but on the church in the modern world. In this sense, the debate on the Second Vatican Council has an inescapable political dimension. Accordingly, looking at post–Vatican II Catholicism is like a theological Rorschach test in which the observer is tempted to project on the screen of the church

[1] Karl Rahner, "The Spirituality of the Church of the Future," in *Theological Investigations*, vol. 20, *Concern for the Church*, trans. Edward Quinn (New York: Crossroad, 1981), 149.
[2] Ibid., 145.

of today his or her ecclesiology, that is, to read the situation of today's church in light of a specific ecclesiological sensibility. This may be one of the reasons that make it impossible today to have a stable and shared historiographical narrative of the post-conciliar period.

Nevertheless, assessing the state of the world and of the church's role in the world is still one of the typical ways of evaluating the trajectories of the council. One indication that all Catholics, including anti-conciliar traditionalists, are in their own way Vatican II Catholics is that the ecclesiology *ad extra* has not remained confined to the theology of the council's enthusiasts. Often heard and repeated criticisms against Vatican II are paradoxically based on an ecclesiology *ad extra* that is clearly inseparable from the very foundations of *Gaudium et Spes*.

Given this correlation between *ad intra* and *ad extra*, and in light of the need to evaluate some of the trajectories of the post–Vatican II period and deal with the open issues for the future of the church, it is necessary as a first step to evaluate the posture and the public role of the Catholic Church in the world of today and especially in democratic societies. It is crucial to take a hard look at the church for what it is in order to avoid the idealization of Vatican II or of the post–Vatican II, which would be no less dangerous than the idealizations of the pre–Vatican II period or the Tridentine period. What follows is a list of six wounds of the post–Vatican II church—list that obviously has no intention of competing with Rosmini's famous *Five Wounds*—one of the works of nineteenth-century Catholic theology that most influenced Vatican II.[3]

1.1 Tribal Catholicism

The Catholic Church is not immune from the *tribalism* of today: a mix of premodern tribalism (based on race, class, power, and gender) and a postmodern tribalism (based on chosen identities or single-issue platforms). For the Catholic Church this means living in an

---

[3] See Antonio Rosmini, *Of the Five Wounds of the Holy Church* (London: Rivington, 1883; original Italian, 1848).

environment that has become more accepting of the idea of "parallel churches"[4] according to the different liturgical and political commitments that divide the church today. It is the postmodern version of the anti-heretical obsession, which is now *à la mode* among the new self-appointed guardians of theological, moral, and liturgical Catholic orthodoxy. This creates a *para-schismatic mentality*, also because of a media culture that fosters the creation of virtual communities disconnected from the concrete experience of the church in its tangible diversities: "This new media ecology threatens the unity of the Church, as it replaces Catholic ecclesial notions of communion with an imported secular model of cultural identity that reduces ritual and doctrine to tools to mark difference. At its extreme, unity is reduced to the mere internal result of the external marking of difference."[5]

This new tribalism is an aberrant form of reception of the fact that the boundaries of the church have become more porous. For this tribal and sectarian mentality, the redefinition of boundaries means not a more welcoming church, a church whose doors are always open to let people in, but a church whose doors are always open to push some people out. The ecclesiology of this mentality dispenses inclusion and exclusion on the basis of ideological renditions of Catholicism and not on the theological and sacramental character of the faithful. The polarization that took place as well in the liturgical life of English-speaking Roman Catholicism during this last decade around the issue of the "extraordinary form" of the Mass and the new English translation of the Missal is part of a larger process of "sorting" within Catholicism beginning with the liturgy (just like Vatican II decided to begin with a document on liturgy).[6]

[4] See Massimo Faggioli, *Sorting Out Catholicism: A Brief History of the New Ecclesial Movements* (Collegeville, MN: Liturgical Press, 2014), 114–17.

[5] Vincent J. Miller, "Ecclesiology, Cultural Change, and the Changing Nature of Culture," in *A Church with Open Doors: Catholic Ecclesiology for the Third Millennium*, ed. Richard R. Gaillardetz and Edward P. Hahnenberg (Collegeville, MN: Liturgical Press, 2015), 82.

[6] See Michael Peppard, "Can the Church Transcend a Polarized Culture?," in *Polarization in the US Catholic Church: Naming the Wounds, Beginning to Heal*, ed. Mary Ellen Konieczny, Charles C. Camosy, and Tricia C. Bruce

1.2. Critical Obedience and Faithful Dissent

The Catholic Church has a problem with *critical obedience and faithful dissent*. Judging from the most vocal member of its hierarchy after the election of Pope Francis, some members of the church apparently no longer know how to be obedient and how to be in dissent. Truth be told, the so-called liberals have long had a problem with obedience. But now that Pope Francis has opened up new spaces, liberals, too, have to learn how to be critically obedient without giving in to the neo-Ultramontanist silencing of those who are disobedient. The so-called conservatives, on the other hand, have long had a problem with dissenters. Now they have to learn how to be faithful in dissent without declaring or hinting that the problem is a pope that does not know Catholic theology or is a heretic. But there is a big difference between these two aisles of western Catholicism. In the years between 1978 and 2005 liberals never thought or insinuated that John Paul II or Benedict XVI were not Catholic or, worse, that they were heretics.

The lost art of critical obedience and faithful dissent may be part of the transition from a mass Catholicism in which everybody is supposedly Catholic and therefore can deal more easily with diversity, to a "minoritarian" Catholicism in which internal diversity is more challenging for the sociological cohesion of the church. In other terms, polarization and the inability to deal with dissent is a consequence of Christianity's loss of hegemony in western civilization. The fact is, though, that Catholicism is the antithesis of sectarianism. Already one century ago Ernst Troeltsch offered very convincing arguments for the sociological and theological differences between church and sect.[7] A deeply changed sociological position within secularized

---

(Collegeville, MN: Liturgical Press, 2016), 151–52. See also Massimo Faggioli, *True Reform: Liturgy and Ecclesiology in* Sacrosanctum Concilium (Collegeville, MN: Liturgical Press, 2012).

[7] See Ernst Troeltsch, *Die Soziallehren der christlichen Kirchen und Gruppen* (Tübingen: Mohr, 1912); English translation: *The Social Teaching of the Christian Churches*, trans. Olive Wyon, with an introductory note by Charles Gore (New York: The Macmillan Company, 1931).

society should not be enough to radically change the way the church deals with differences of opinion that are within the domain of what is open to debate and change. The real root of this mutation is not necessitated by the transition from majority to minority, but it is a consequence of the "ideologization" of Catholicism in which the culture of debate and dissent is repressed.

The deeply underlying issue is ecclesiological, and it is no coincidence that there are differences within global Catholicism. The ruthless use of power by some bishops in the English-speaking world in shutting down ecclesial initiatives or silencing individual theologians or priests or nuns is mostly unknown in many other parts of the world. That is especially true in the smaller and younger churches of Asia, for example, where Catholicism never was the sociological, political, or cultural majority. The Catholic Church is still learning to operate in an environment of "communicative dissent," in society at large and within the church.[8]

1.3. Catholicism and Culturalism

It is a church that has become *overly concerned with culture*. There is no question that at Vatican II culture became a *locus theologicus*.[9] "Culture" and "cultural" are mentioned and referred to eighty-five times in the corpus of Vatican II.[10] But what Vatican II meant for "culture" was different from what it has become recently. In his December 6, 1962, address at the council Cardinal Giacomo Lercaro

---

[8] See Franz-Xaver Kaufmann, *Kirche in der ambivalenten Moderne* (Freiburg i.Br.: Herder, 2012), 170–78.

[9] See Elmar Salmann, *Presenza di spirito. Il cristianesimo come stile di pensiero e di vita*, ed. Armando Matteo (Assisi: Cittadella, 2011), 282–84. For culture as a *locus theologicus* for theological hermeneutics in the post-conciliar church, see the lifelong reflection by Peter Hünermann, *Dogmatische Prinzipienlehre: Glaube, Überlieferung, Theologie als Sprach- und Wahrheitsgeschehen* (Münster: Aschendorff, 2003), and recently *Sprache des Glaubens—Sprache des Lehramts—Sprache der Theologie. Eine geschichtliche Orientierung* (Freiburg i.Br.: Herder, 2015).

[10] See Peter Hünermann, ed., *Die Dokumente des Zweiten Vatikanischen Konzils. Zweisprachige Studienausgabe* (Freiburg i.Br.: Herder, 2012), 866.

talked about the need for the church "to be culturally 'poor,'"[11] meaning that the glorious traditions of Catholicism should not limit the universality of the church's language, should not divide rather than unite, should not repel many more men and women than they attract and convince.

In recent times, the main worry of some leading Catholic pastoral and intellectual leaders became an emphasis on culture. For them it is about *reculturation* of the West, in order to avoid *exculturation* of Christianity from culture.[12] It is not anymore about *inculturation*, as it used to be during the early post–Vatican II period: this late twentieth-century and early twenty-first-century culturalism starts for the most part from a very western understanding of Catholic culture in terms of Western European and North American white culture (singular) as the standard.

We did not see this only in the "culture wars" in the United States. In Italy, too, during the 1990s the landmark initiative of the Italian bishops' conference under its leader, Cardinal Camillo Ruini (1986–2007), was for a "cultural project oriented in Christian direction": this project never really took off after its launch in 1997 and had no impact on Italian culture, not even on the culture of Italian Catholics, except for some public lectures and academic conferences.

The church is certainly a place for the encounter of different cultures. But when this emphasis on culture (in the singular) is not an emphasis on education, on the role of spiritual life and of theological reflection, this culturalism is the vehicle for the temptation of integrism. For this culturalism, culture is a new language for talking about hegemony, expressing the dream of a new *christianitas*, of Christendom, as well as the illusion of finding the common space a

---

[11] See Giuseppe Ruggieri, "Beyond an Ecclesiology of Polemics," in *History of Vatican II*, ed. Giuseppe Alberigo, English edition by Joseph A. Komonchak, vol. 2, *The Formation of the Council's Identity, First Period and Intercession, October 1962–September 1963* (Maryknoll, NY: Orbis Books; Leuven: Peeters, 1997), 345–47.

[12] About the concept of "exculturation," see Danièle Hervieu-Léger, *Catholicisme, la fin d'un monde* (Paris: Bayard, 2003).

theologically empty space, thus minimizing the role of Jesus Christ in the specificity of Christianity.[13]

The church as a merely cultural agent (or, even worse, as a cultural warrior) reduces Catholicism to one culture among many cultures; it does not see theology as relevant as a marker for the visibility of Catholicism; it fosters a separation between theology and church leaders and the formation of future ministers. One of the paradoxes of this emphasis on culture is the undeniable marginalization of Catholic theological thinking from the public square, which is also due to the persisting clericalism of formation in the church despite the fact that in these last fifty years doing theology is no longer a monopoly of the clergy. There is a clear cognitive dissonance between the church's recent emphasis on culture and the insisted reliance on clerical culture as the knowledge of the church.

1.4. Catholics and Freedom

It is a church that has a *problem with freedom*. Since Vatican II, religious freedom has become part of the conscience of Catholicism worldwide, but this church clearly still struggles with the idea that religious freedom is for all—Catholics, non-Catholics, and non-Christians as well where Catholicism is (or used to be) the established religion or the religion of the vast majority (as in Europe and North America). It is a church that has not decided yet if the history of the church wants to be part of the history of freedom.

These doubts about freedom are caused by the experience of the post-conciliar period, when Catholicism liberated itself from the precisely demarcated cultural canon of the *societas perfecta*. At Vatican II the church talked about freedom of conscience and became a powerful global advocate for democracy and the respect of civil and political rights of Catholics and non-Catholics. Today the sociological decline of Catholicism is still framed in terms of

---

[13] About this, see Piero Coda, *Il Concilio della Misericordia. Sui sentieri del Vaticano II*, ed. Alessandro Clemenzia and Julie Tremblay (Rome: Città Nuova, 2015), 301–12.

the price paid for an overly optimistic assessment of the impact of freedom on religion. These worries for the consequences of the embrace of freedom on the unity and strength of the church have caused in neo-conservative Catholic circles a growing skepticism about the compatibility between Catholicism and liberal pluralistic democracy. This skepticism is not articulated in the desire to return to a predemocratic era; rather, it is expressed in the aspiration to reconstruct the church in a separate world in which the political dimension would be somehow magically absent.

In the early 1990s Samuel Huntington stated that in the post–Vatican II period, Catholicism became a driving force for democratic revolutions all over the world, for changes that had happened at two different levels: Vatican II and its "political" message (social change, collegiality, rights of individuals, common good), and base-popular involvement (basic ecclesial communities in Brazil, Christian Left in the Philippines, grassroots politicization of the church in Poland, Argentina, and Chile).[14] It is worth asking how Huntington would amend his analysis in light of the changes in the attitudes of Catholics (including the institutional church) toward democracy during this last decade: not only in countries with a considerable Catholic presence in which democracy is in crisis (such as Poland, Hungary, and the Philippines), but also in those countries in which the politics of Catholics (especially of the Catholic intelligentsia) is marked by a sense of fatalism because of the inevitability of the demise of the democratic system now held prisoner or made irrelevant by capitalistic globalization.

1.5. Catholicism and the Secular

It is a church that has to readdress its *relationship with the secular*. In particular, there is a gap between Europe and North America about the role of the secular for the church. Since the mid-twentieth century European Catholicism has developed a theology of *secularity*

---

[14] See Samuel P. Huntington, *The Third Wave: Democratization in the Late Twentieth Century* (Norman: University of Oklahoma Press, 1991), 72–85.

in terms of distinction, of the opening of new spaces for the church, of overlapping spaces in a world in which individuals have multiple identities: a theology of secularity different from a theology of *secularization*.[15] On the other side of the Atlantic, the idea and the praxis of Catholicism toward the secular in the ecclesial language in North America looks through the theological eyes of a European Catholic as overly militant, early twentieth-century, pre–Vatican II.[16]

It is not just an issue of ecclesial posture or language of the magisterium, but also of the political culture of Catholics as citizens. The intellectual discourse on the "post-secular" is often a discourse not just against secularism, but against secularity itself, sometimes in terms of an anti-secular front. This is not the post-secular that Charles Taylor had in mind, that is, the post-secular as "a time in which the hegemony of the mainstream master narrative of secularization will be more and more challenged."[17] Secularization, secularism, and secularity are related to one another, but are different concepts that require different theological analysis: this is important for understanding the relations between the North American political-religious perspective on the one side and the secular and post-secular in the world of today on the other side.[18] But it is also crucial in order to deal with the North American religious landscape of today: the emergence of the so-called "nones" has certainly to do with the secularization of western societies, but the "nones" have more to do with the porousness between religiosity, spirituality, and secularity than with an old-style ideological secularism.

---

[15] About this, see Lois Lee, *Recognizing the Non-Religious: Reimagining the Secular* (New York: Oxford University Press, 2015).

[16] For a European perspective, see *Teologia nella città, teologia per la città. La dimensione secolare delle scienze teologiche*, ed. Antonio Autiero (Bologna: EDB, 2005).

[17] Charles Taylor, *A Secular Age* (Cambridge, MA: Harvard University Press, 2007), 534.

[18] See *Toward a Postsecular International Relations: New Forms of Community, Identity, and Power*, ed. Luca Mavelli and Fabio Petito (New York: Palgrave Macmillan, 2014).

1.6. Insiders or Outsiders?

The Catholic Church still struggles with the false alternative between *insiders or outsiders*: insiders of a national/mainstream culture, natural-born insiders or finally accepted by the cultural gatekeepers, versus outsiders in the sense of a new moral and religious minority, outvoted on life issues and sexual morality issues or leaving the mainstream looking for a new credible outsiderhood. These are no longer mutually exclusive alternatives. It is a church that knows that we live in an age in which the boundaries between the inside and the outside of the sacred are no longer defined by the church and the inside and the outside of the political are not defined by states and governments. But it is a church that still struggles to see itself beyond that age.

On the one hand we have a church that speaks the language of the outsider when it feels outvoted but retains the privileges of the insider when it can. In this sense, the so-called "Benedict option" is the illusion of the possibility of withdrawal in the attempt to become outsiders again vis-à-vis "the world" outside, and the attempt to recreate on the inside, in smaller communities, a majority complex.[19] On the other side, we have the split between an "insiderist" Catholicism that requires Catholics to defer to American civil religion in terms of unchecked nationalism and militarism, versus Catholics that reject American exceptionalism and with it also the legitimacy of the nation-state as one of the keepers of the common good.[20]

2. From Vatican II to Pope Francis's Vision for the Church

The cure for these wounds in post–Vatican II Catholicism is not a return to a previous moment in the timeline of the church through

---

[19] About this, see Gerald W. Schlabach, "The Virtue of Staying Put: What the 'Benedict Option' Forgets about Benedictines," *Commonweal* (October 7, 2016): 11–13.

[20] See, for example, William T. Cavanaugh, *Migrations of the Holy: God, State, and the Political Meaning of the Church* (Grand Rapids, MI: Eerdmans, 2011).

outright rejection of the reforms of the post-conciliar period or the ambiguous reduction of Vatican II to a merely pastoral, nondoctrinal council. The ecclesiology of Vatican II is vital for global Catholicism today: there is an overlay between the fundamental reorientation of Catholic theology at Vatican II and the theological reorientation of the Catholic Church under Pope Francis. Jorge Mario Bergoglio is one of the fruits of Vatican II, and it is not a coincidence that the opposition to the council as a moment of change in the church is at the basis of and largely coincides with the opposition to Pope Francis.

Vatican II is still necessary also for an ecclesiology of the Catholic Church in the public square, and a new appropriation of Vatican II is at the heart of how Pope Francis uses the council, especially for ecclesiology. This has become clear since the beginning of his pontificate. The foundational document of Francis's pontificate, the apostolic exhortation *Evangelii Gaudium*, offered a first magisterial explanation of the ecclesiology of his pontificate. An important part is at paragraph 236, right after the four axioms that are the philosophical key to Francis's worldview (par. 232–37): *time is greater than space* (eschatological horizon); *unity prevails over conflict* (the idea of process: from conflict to a superior level of mediation); *realities are more important than ideas* (from metaphysics to phenomenology); *the whole is greater than the part* (what is partial and what is universal).

In paragraph 236 Francis explains his ecclesiological model with the geometric figure of the polyhedron:

> Here our model is not the sphere, which is no greater than its parts, where every point is equidistant from the centre, and there are no differences between them. Instead, it is the polyhedron, which reflects the convergence of all its parts, each of which preserves its distinctiveness. Pastoral and political activity alike seek to gather in this polyhedron the best of each. There is a place for the poor and their culture, their aspirations and their potential. Even people who can be considered dubious on account of their errors have something to offer which must not be overlooked. It is the convergence of peoples who, within the universal order, maintain their own individuality; it is the sum total of persons within a society

which pursues the common good, which truly has a place for everyone.

Francis's polyhedron is the union of all the different subparts, in a description that overcomes the centralistic understanding of the relations between the center and the peripheries.[21] It is an essential part of the ecclesiology of Francis, based on a mystic vision of the people, on discernment as an antidote to ideology, and on the idea of change, in the church as well, as a process dealing with conflicts, contradictions, tensions, and temptations.[22]

The other key ecclesiological emphasis in *Evangelii Gaudium* is about mercy, which is the most important hermeneutical key to interpreting the whole pontificate.

> The Church which "goes forth" is a community of missionary disciples who take the first step, who are involved and supportive, who bear fruit and rejoice. An evangelizing community knows that the Lord has taken the initiative, he has loved us first (cf. *1 Jn* 4:19), and therefore we can move forward, boldly take the initiative, go out to others, seek those who have fallen away, stand at the crossroads and welcome the outcast. Such a community has an endless desire to show mercy, the fruit of its own experience of the power of the Father's infinite mercy. (EG 24)

Evangelii Gaudium quotes John XXIII's opening speech of Vatican II (EG 84). But after *Evangelii Gaudium*, too, Francis has stressed the parallels between John XXIII and himself. The Bull of Indiction

---

[21] See Pavulraj Michael, "Una lettura ermeneutica sul discernimento pastorale in *Evangelii Gaudium*: le sfide e le risposte," in Evangelii Gaudium: *il testo ci interroga*, ed. Humberto Miguel Yanez (Rome: Gregorian & Biblical Press, 2014), 109–24.

[22] About this, see Antonio Spadaro, "La riforma della Chiesa secondo Francesco. Le radici ignaziane," and Carlos Maria Galli, "La riforma della chiesa secondo Francesco. L'ecclesiologia del popolo di Dio," in *La riforma e le riforme nella chiesa*, ed. Antonio Spadaro and Carlos Maria Galli (Brescia: Queriniana, 2016), 9–26 and 27–55.

of the Extraordinary Jubilee of Mercy (*Misericordiae Vultus*, April 11, 2015) quoted once again from John XXIII's opening speech of Vatican II, *Gaudet Mater Ecclesia*:

> I have chosen the date of 8 December because of its rich meaning in the recent history of the church. In fact, I will open the Holy Door on the fiftieth anniversary of the closing of the Second Vatican Ecumenical Council. The Church feels a great need to keep this event alive. With the Council, the Church entered a new phase of her history. The Council Fathers strongly perceived, as a true breath of the Holy Spirit, a need to talk about God to men and women of their time in a more accessible way. The walls which for too long had made the Church a kind of fortress were torn down and the time had come to proclaim the Gospel in a new way. It was a new phase of the same evangelization that had existed from the beginning. It was a fresh undertaking for all Christians to bear witness to their faith with greater enthusiasm and conviction. The Church sensed a responsibility to be a living sign of the Father's love in the world. We recall the poignant words of Saint John XXIII when, opening the Council, he indicated the path to follow: "Now the Bride of Christ wishes to use the medicine of mercy rather than taking up arms of severity. . . . The Catholic Church, as she holds high the torch of Catholic truth at this Ecumenical Council, wants to show herself a loving mother to all; patient, kind, moved by compassion and goodness toward her separated children."[23]

Francis's ecclesiology is deeply rooted in Vatican II and in the development of the theology on the church in the twentieth century. Particularly important for Francis is the thought of Erich Przywara for the analysis of the relationship between the Catholic Church

---

[23] Pope Francis, *Misericordiae Vultus* (April 11, 2015), par. 4, http://w2 .vatican.va/content/francesco/en/apost_letters/documents/papa-francesco _bolla_20150411_misericordiae-vultus.html.

and the legacy of European Christendom.[24] But not less radical is Francis's use of Przywara for the analysis of the intra-ecclesial ideological distortions and relativizations at the core of Christianity.[25] The way Francis talks about the church in *Evangelii Gaudium* is not disconnected from the concrete ecclesiology of the pontificate, which offers a vision for the church of the near future. This vision can be summarized in four points:

1) the church in the trajectories from Vatican II to the twenty-first century

2) "Roman" Catholicism in the global world of today

3) a church beyond political-ideological alignments

4) contextuality for an ecclesiology of mercy

2.1. The Church in the Trajectories from Vatican II to the Twenty-First Century

The ecclesiological trajectories of Vatican II develop during the period between the celebration of the council and today, with different phases but with no real interruption. A particular moment in this process is Pope Francis's pontificate. Francis is a post-conciliar pope with a biographically unproblematic and theologically resolved relationship with the council, which he sees not as part of an autobiographical or ideological narrative, but as part of the Catholic tradition. Francis's polyhedron and the overall ecclesiology of *Evangelii Gaudium* are an imaginative and creative reception of the main trajectories of Catholic ecclesiology since Vatican II for a missionary church. This reception comprises a few fundamental shifts for a vision of the church of the future.

---

[24] See Antonio Spadaro, "La diplomazia di Francesco. La misericordia come processo politico," *La Civiltà Cattolica* 3975 (February 13, 2015): 209–26; Erich Przywara, *L'idea d'Europa. La "crisi" di ogni politica "cristiana"*, ed. Fabrizio Mandreoli and José Luis Narvaja (Torino: Il pozzo di Giacobbe, 2013).

[25] See José Luis Narvaja, "L'eresia intraecclesiale," *La Civiltà Cattolica* 3992 (October 22, 2016): 105–13.

There is the shift *from a Eurocentric church to a global church*: it is the church in the modern world of the pastoral constitution *Gaudium et Spes*: world in the historical sense of the world of this time and in the geographical sense of global world. This entails not just a decentralization of the church from Europe, but also a reconsideration of the new evangelization, which in this last quarter of a century counted more on new actors of evangelization than on a new model of evangelization.[26] The ecclesiology of the church in the modern world means a new approach to the relationship between parishes (territorial/diocesan church) and ecclesial movements. This will also mean a new appraisal of the necessary gap between the ideal of Catholic "intentional communities" and the complicated reality of communities of people who cannot and will not commit to an intentional community. In *Evangelii Gaudium* (par. 28–29) Francis spoke clearly about the need to find a new balance between territorial church and movements/communities.[27]

There is the shift *from a church as institution/establishment to a church in mission*. This means not just the end of an institutional ecclesiocentrism, but also the end of the illusion that a bureaucratic modernization of the church and a streamlining of its processes can enable the church to be missionary. An ecclesiological shift from a church based on "identity" (in German: from *Wer-Identität*) to a church based on "where it stands" (in German: *Wo-Frage*)[28] requires a new way of thinking and of acting, and a new dynamism of pastoral ministry. Francis's vision and action for the reform of the institutions of the church is rooted not in an institutional rationale,

---

[26] See Stephen Bevans, "Beyond the New Evangelization: Toward a Missionary Ecclesiology for the Twenty-First Century," in *A Church with Open Doors: Ecclesiology for the Third Millennium*, ed. Richard R. Gaillardetz and Edward P. Hahnenberg (Collegeville, MN: Liturgical Press, 2015), 3–22, esp. 8–10.

[27] About this, see Massimo Faggioli, *The Rising Laity: Ecclesial Movements since Vatican II* (Mahwah, NJ: Paulist Press, 2016).

[28] See Hans-Joachim Sander, "Theologischer Kommentar zur Pastoralkonstitution über die Kirche in der Welt von heute," in *Herders Theologischer Kommentar zum Zweiten Vatikanischen Konzil*, ed. Bernd Jochen Hilberath and Peter Hünermann, vol. 5 (Freiburg i.B: Herder, 2005), 696–98.

but in a missionary urgency.[29] This will also have consequences for the institutional structure of the church, including the Vatican and the Roman Curia.[30]

There is the shift *from a sociological and cultural Catholicism to an inclusive church*. This shift finally questions the too obvious identification between Catholicism and European and western society, an identification that has produced moralistic assumptions about Christianity and about Catholicism. This shift about inclusion is not only about changing the size and shape of the church, but also about changing its dynamic and inspecting its *Christlichkeit*, that is, its Christian character. This must happen also at the local level, where the liturgical life of the community is called to express an inclusive and ecumenical ecclesiology (as well as in terms of what I would call intra-Catholic ecumenism), especially in light of the recent polarization around the liturgy: "a determined pastoral effort to keep the liturgy, above all, from becoming a battleground for confrontation and polarization."[31] The liturgy cannot become just the symbolic marker of the Christian community, as Francis said in *Evangelii Gaudium*: "In some people we see an ostentatious preoccupation for the liturgy, for doctrine and for the Church's prestige, but without any concern that the Gospel have a real impact on God's faithful people and the concrete needs of the present time" (EG 95).

Inclusion for Francis means especially inclusion of the poor. From Vatican II comes the *shift to a church of the poor*, in a radical acceptance of the call of the council to read the "signs of the times" (GS 4) for a church that wants to be *servant et pauvre*, servant and poor.[32] In order to understand the importance of *Gaudium et Spes*

---

[29] See Spadaro, "La riforma della Chiesa secondo Francesco. Le radici ignaziane."

[30] See the article by Bishop Marcello Semeraro (secretary of the council of cardinals created by Pope Francis), "La riforma di papa Francesco," *Il Regno—attualità* 14 (July 15, 2016): 433–41.

[31] Common Ground Initiative, *Called to Be Catholic*, section 4, http://www.catholiccommonground.org/called-be-catholic.

[32] See Yves Congar, *Pour une Église servante et pauvre* (Paris: Cerf, 1963). New editions published in French in 2014; in Italian by the Community of

for Francis it is necessary to see the ecclesiology of the pastoral constitution also as the completion of a theological discourse that at Vatican II begins with the council fathers' *Message to the World* (drafted by Marie-Dominique Chenu) of October 20, 1962: "It is far from true that because we cling to Christ we are diverted from earthly duties and toils. On the contrary, faith, hope, and the love of Christ impel us to serve our brothers, thereby patterning ourselves after the example of the Divine Teacher, who 'came not to be served but to serve' (Mt. 20:28). Hence, the church too was not born to dominate but to serve. He laid down His life for us, and we too ought to lay down our lives for our brothers (1 Jn. 3:16)."[33]

2.2. "Roman" Catholicism in the Global World of Today

One possible answer to the challenges of freedom and of lost insiderhood is a renewed appreciation of the particular role of *Roman* Catholicism in the global world. The ecclesiological trajectories of Vatican II cannot be understood separately from the permanence of something distinctive in the institutional and political genius of Roman Catholicism. The periodization and the distinction between "conciliar" and "post-conciliar" Catholicism is not yet stable in the historical and theological literature. But there is no doubt that there are phenomena that are truly post-conciliar, such as the rise of political Islam and the new relationship between religion, secularity, and nationalism vs. internationalism perceived as capitalistic globalization. The council's ecclesiology interacts with new issues in a rapidly changed scenario.

The first change is in the relations between the role of Catholicism and democratic *ethos*. The world of the early twenty-first century is significantly different from the world of the 1960s, when

---

Bose, *Per una chiesa serva e povera* (Magnano, 2014); and in English, *Power and Poverty in the Church: The Renewal and Understanding of Service* (Mahwah, NJ: Paulist Press, 2016). These new editions make clear the importance of Congar's ecclesiology for the pontificate of Francis.

[33] Vatican II, "Message to Humanity," in *The Documents of Vatican II*, ed. Walter M. Abbott (New York: Guild Press, 1966), 4–5.

the acceptance of democracy by the Catholic Church coincided with the hopes for a global world in which transition to democracy was assumed to be part of the social and economic development of peoples and nations. Fifty years later, the equivalence and causal connection between democracy and development, between democracy and capitalism is in crisis, because it is clear that capitalism and economic development can thrive without democracy and respect of human rights.

Particularly relevant in this scenario is the permanence of the global role of the Catholic Church—one of the proofs of the decline of the secularization thesis, even though the church's role and visibility do not necessarily mean influence. In *Evangelii Gaudium* par. 236 Francis's polyhedron expresses an ecclesiology that is not shy about the particular role of Catholicism as global force: Francis writes of how "pastoral and political activity alike seek to gather in this polyhedron the best of each."

In a world in which religion means largely deinstitutionalized religions, Catholicism in the twenty-first century still works a great deal at the institutional and universal levels: "Catholicism has a long historical memory, so it knows better than to identify current circumstances with eternal truths. It is international, so it has resources for getting beyond parochially American categories and patterns. It has resources in Catholic theology and ethics that challenge simple left/right binaries."[34] In this sense, the "Roman" part of Roman Catholicism is more relevant than most Catholics (including many Catholic theologians) think. Politically speaking, the Vatican is a relic of the past that owes more to the political history of Europe than to the martyrdom of Paul and Peter. But there is a resilience of that place, its symbolism, and its ability to recognize and interpret world events, that is the fruit of the church's ability to adapt to changed conditions. In 1870 the papacy lost Rome and temporal power, but after Vatican II Paul VI called the loss of temporal power providential (in a complete

[34] David P. Gushee, "Left/Right Polarization as Culture Wars Captivity: One Scholar's Journey and Analysis," in Konieczny et al., *Polarization in the US Catholic Church*, 87.

reversal of what Pius IX had said in the *Syllabus of Errors* of 1864). With John Paul II and Benedict XVI the Vatican became the center of church politics in the sense of centralization in Rome of the decision-making processes in the global Catholic Church. Under Francis, Rome is the springboard for a synodal and collegial church and for a church that is not wedded to Europe or to a particular culture: the synodal process of 2014–2015 was important for the new impulse it gave to the relationship between Catholic teaching on marriage and global Catholicism and between papal teaching, episcopal collegiality, and synodality to the whole people of God.[35]

In this particular moment, for a church like the Roman Catholic Church that still struggles to reform itself in a way that makes it less dependent on the political-institutional legacy of the clash between the papacy and the empire in the Middle Ages, it is important for the church to cherish the virtues of an ecclesial system of governance that does not always need to become procedural. After World War II, Catholicism embraced the democratic system as the system that is compatible with the respect of human dignity. The global Catholic Church cannot be antidemocratic anymore, but it still has the luxury and responsibility to be not democratic, in order to serve the common good in a world in which the crisis of democratic systems is affecting the prospects of a great number of men and women. But the nondemocratic governance of the Catholic Church (and all the dangerous spiritualizations that come to explain that system) cannot become an alibi for the depoliticization of Catholic citizenship:

> People in every nation enhance the social dimension of their lives by acting as committed and responsible citizens, not as a mob swayed by the powers that be. Let us not forget that "responsible citizenship is a virtue, and participation in political life is a moral obligation" [United States Conference

---

[35] The most important papal text on collegiality and synodality in the post-conciliar period is Francis's address at the ceremony commemorating the fiftieth anniversary of the institution of the Synod of Bishops, October 17, 2015, http:// w2.vatican.va/content/francesco/en/speeches/2015/october/documents/papa -francesc_20151017_50-anniversario-sinodo.html.

of Catholic Bishops, Pastoral Letter *Forming Conscience for Faithful Citizenship* [November 2007], 13]. Yet becoming a people demands something more. It is an ongoing process in which every new generation must take part: a slow and arduous effort calling for a desire for integration and a willingness to achieve this through the growth of a peaceful and multifaceted culture of encounter. (EG 220)

2.3. A Church Beyond the Political-Ideological Alignments

The issues with obedience/dissent and with a culturalist interpretation of Catholicism cannot be solved without understanding the tension between the ecclesiology of Vatican II and recent ideological manipulations of Catholicism. The Roman element within Roman Catholicism is key to remembering how uncharacteristic and transient are the ideological alignments within western Catholicism in these last few decades. Catholicism has gone through different political-theological alignments during this last century: first the anti-Communist front (from the early twentieth century until John Paul II), then the biopolitical fault-line (beginning in the 1960s and especially in 1968 with Paul VI's encyclical *Humanae Vitae*) about the life issues.[36] Forging an ideological alignment for Catholicism today would require an alliance shaped by an intellectual and moral convergence on the issues of technocratic globalization, climate change, populism threatening democracy, and religiously inspired violence.

Francis's ecclesiology clearly challenges the ideological alignments formed within western Catholicism in the late twentieth and early twenty-first centuries. The pontificate of Pope Francis on the one hand and the crisis of ideological alignments in America (and not only) on the other hand are concrete evidence of the end of an era

---

[36] See Stephen R. Schloesser, "'Dancing on the Edge of the Volcano': Biopolitics and What Happened after Vatican II," in *From Vatican II to Pope Francis: Charting a Catholic Future*, ed. Paul Crowley (Maryknoll, NY: Orbis Books, 2014), 3–26.

both in American and western politics and in the church. There is a clear parallel between the crisis of American political-religious ideologies and the divisions among US Catholics. The crisis of political conservatism is part of the crisis within the political culture of the Catholic leadership in these last thirty years. This is evident in the United States of America, but it is a more general crisis. What is happening now in America happened in a similar way in Italy in the early 1960s with John XXIII, whose pontificate (and his decision to call the Second Vatican Council) led to a reassessment of the apparently unavoidable alliance between a Catholic party and the political center-right in post–World War II Italy. On a smaller scale, it happened also in the post–John Paul II and post–Benedict XVI period in Italy, where the establishment of the political right wing basically ceased to exist without ecclesiastical life support.[37]

Francis's ecclesiology and his whole pontificate is a resetting of the political alignments within Catholicism: there is a change in the global perspective of the first non-European pope, but there is also a genuine ecclesiological shift in *Evangelii Gaudium*. From this point of view, the year 2013, with the election of Jorge Mario Bergoglio as Pope Francis, marks the definitive end of a certain type of geopolitical and geo-religious world map: Rome is the epicenter of this tectonic shift; the United States of America and American Catholicism is where the impact of these moving tectonic plates is felt more than anywhere else, both politically and ecclesially.[38]

2.4. Contextuality for an Ecclesiology of Mercy

The challenges coming from Catholic tribalism and from secularity must be seen from the point of view of the new contextualization of the church today. Paradoxically, at this time the recontextualization of Catholicism started from its symbolical center, from Rome. One

---

[37] See Marco Ventura, *Creduli e credenti: Il declino di Stato e Chiesa come questione di fede* (Turin: Einaudi, 2014).

[38] See Massimo Faggioli, *Pope Francis: Tradition in Transition* (Mahwah, NJ: Paulist Press, 2015).

of the most important contributions of Francis's ecclesiology is about a *recontextualization* of Catholic theology and doctrine, beginning with a recontextualization and reinculturation of the Roman papacy.

In Francis we have a papacy that is not less visible and prominent, in the church and in the world, than was the case with his predecessors. It is an understatement to say that the papacy is not immune from the temptations of giving visibility to the Roman center at the expenses of the real church: there is a connection (to be researched) between the new visibility of papacy during this last century and the Catholic virtualization of reality. But it is a papacy being resignified now by a pope with a profoundly different experience as a priest and as a bishop. One of the most perceptive interpreters of our time, French philosopher and sociologist Jean Baudrillard (1929–2007), talked about a society made of "simulacra."[39] The simulacra system is a system of signs that allow society to work, but that can also be detached from concrete reality. Speed is an integral part of the "simulacra society" because the ability to do many more things, thanks to technology, implies *deresponsibilization*. In theological language and for the life of the church, this kind of culture of simulacra carries within itself the risk of a radical "de-incarnation" typical of relationships that are more virtual than real (as it is the case with social networks on the internet). Pope Francis entered the simulacra system of our society through the postmodern door of global media, but he does it in order to *reincarnate* the Gospel in concrete relationships.

This virtualization is best visible in the new role played by the Catholic blogosphere. Militant blogs and militant religious media have reinforced an individualized concept of the Christian experience, with an ecclesiological effect of division within the community. But this also has a theological side that is much more persistent and influential than the myriad of Catholic blogs. The virtualization of Catholicism in the theological sense means the weakening of the voice of local churches and a *decontextualization* of their position in the universal church.

---

[39] See Jean Baudrillard, *Simulacra and Simulation*, trans. Sheila Faria Glaser (Ann Arbor: University of Michigan Press, 1994).

The emphasis on mercy must be seen as part of a new contextualization of theology against the politically expedient tendency to decontextualize the Church and theology.[40] Contextualization means breaking a political taboo thanks to the two key words of his pontificate: the poor and mercy. Being poor has become not a social-economic condition, but a heresy proving false the universal promise of wealth: talking about the poor therefore challenges not only assumptions about the use of tax money or allocation of resources, but also the political-religious identity of a gentrified Catholicism that would like to make Jesus Christ a self-righteous moralist.

The emphasis on mercy, on the other hand, violates the "law and order" mentality of the self-appointed guardians of Catholic orthodoxy. Catholicism is not unchangeable doctrine that cannot be contaminated by theological developments and by the idea of the pastorality of doctrine. Francis responded to this kind of criticism with one of his most impressive speeches, the one on October 24, 2015, at the end of the Synod. The Synod, said Francis, "was about bearing witness to everyone that, for the church, the Gospel continues to be a vital source of eternal newness, against all those who would 'indoctrinate' it in dead stones to be hurled at others. It was also about laying closed hearts, which bare the closed hearts which frequently hide even behind the church's teachings or good intentions, in order to sit in the chair of Moses and judge, sometimes with superiority and superficiality, difficult cases and wounded families."[41]

[40] One of the sources of inspiration for Francis was Walter Kasper, *Mercy: The Essence of the Gospel and the Key to Christian Life* (Mahwah, NJ: Paulist Press, 2014).

[41] Francis, speech for the conclusion of the Ordinary Synod on the family, October 24, 2015, http://w2.vatican.va/content/francesco/en/speeches/2015/october/documents/papa-francesco_20151024_sinodo-conclusione-lavori.html. Francis has repeated his vision of the relationship between Christian faith and ideologization of doctrines very often in his homilies during the morning Mass he celebrates every day in Santa Marta. One example, the homily of October 6, 2016, http://it.radio vaticana.va/news/2016/10/06/il_papa_presiede_la_messa_a_santa_marta/1263214.

3. Toward an Ecclesiology of Mercy

Francis's emphasis of mercy in his whole pontificate has an ecclesiological potential that the church should not waste. An ecclesiology of mercy responds to the needs of a missionary, inclusive, nonideological, engaged, and contextual church.

Italian theologian Stella Morra cast a light on the consequences of mercy for theology and for the church in a compelling way. Morra points out that the emphasis on mercy answers the question of whether Christianity is an abstract intellectual truth or a form of life. Mercy can change the way the church deals with reality, not only on the linguistic level (how we talk about things), but also on the practical level (how we deal with things) and especially on the ritual level (how we make of the act of mercy a sacramental act that gives grace). Mercy can only be relational; it is not an object or an idea; it changes all subjects involved; it is not subject to doctrinal definition; is practical and experiential; it is always transcendent, in the sense that every act of mercy has to do with the divine; it is by definition inclusive and cannot be used to shape an exclusive, identity-obsessed form of the Christian faith. One of the most important facts is that there is no particular minister of mercy; rather, we are all ministers of mercy. For example, a person does not need to be a priest to "perform" the seven works of corporal mercy (feed the hungry, give drink to the thirsty, clothe the naked, shelter the homeless, care for the sick, visit the imprisoned, bury the dead) or the seven works of spiritual mercy (share knowledge, give advice to those who need it, comfort the suffering, be patient with others, forgive those who hurt you, give correction to those who need it, pray for the living and the dead). In all these works the "matter" of the sacrament of mercy is life itself, and the ministers are each one of us.[42]

It is necessary now to accompany the transition from a spiritual and sacramental discourse on mercy to the ecclesiological level. Mercy is process, and an ecclesiology of mercy means a church in

---

[42] For the ecclesiological and theological consequences of mercy, see Stella Morra, *Dio non si stanca. La misericordia come forma ecclesiale* (Bologna: EDB, 2015), 61–62 and 101–32.

process. This ecclesiology of mercy would change the church's praxis, beginning to heal also the wounds I mentioned earlier, beginning with a corrective to the underestimation of Christian practices and to the evaluation of them only in terms of correct application of a correct theory.

The ecclesiology of mercy opens many spaces for a renewed church. This renewed church need not obsess about continuity versus discontinuity, or about magisterium versus theology, or spirit versus institution. Francis's pontificate—what Francis is and says—offers a new vision for the future of the Catholic Church:

> Being Church means being God's people, in accordance with the great plan of his fatherly love. This means that we are to be God's leaven in the midst of humanity. It means proclaiming and bringing God's salvation into our world, which often goes astray and needs to be encouraged, given hope and strengthened on the way. The Church must be a place of mercy freely given, where everyone can feel welcomed, loved, forgiven and encouraged to live the good life of the Gospel. (EG 114)

Conclusion

With this project I wanted to warn against the dangers of the temptation to establish the "city of God" within the "earthly city." This book makes several references to Augustine, but the reflections in this book cannot solve the problem of the role of political Augustinianism in English-speaking Catholicism today, and especially in the United States. This is an issue that would need more in-depth historical and theological analysis, and a series of comparative studies about different ecclesiologies and different kinds of Augustinianism in post–Vatican II magisterium and theology, in different parts of the world and of global Catholicism.

For now this book tries to make a case for the necessity of looking at the issue of the role of Catholicism in the public square today from an historical-theological perspective that needs to be aware of and take into serious consideration the importance of pre-medieval and pre-Christendom times as well as a late modern and post-Christendom perspective. This is one of the unfinished projects of Vatican II: a theological *ressourcement* aimed at a reconsideration of the whole Catholic tradition (including Vatican I and Trent), in order to overcome the default approach to the past, that is, looking at medieval Christendom as *the* past to which Roman Catholics supposedly ought to refer as the standard and the golden age.

From my experience as a European Catholic who moved to America in 2008 and has taught and written for the American Catholic Academy and the public at large since then, I believe it is impossible to overestimate the influence of the Catholic medieval imagination in the social and cultural imagination of American Catholicism. It is powerful and has many consequences, not just for the architecture of college campuses in the United States, but also and especially for the perception of what "the world" is to the eyes of the Catholic Church in the United States.[1] Beyond the theological canon that spans the centuries between Augustine and Thomas Aquinas, there seems to be a lot of room for both antimodernism and postmodernism, but very little room for what theology is between the early modern period (Erasmus included) and the *nouvelle théologie* leading to the Second Vatican Council. Whoever won the "cultural wars," Vatican II was collateral damage.

This had consequences for the intellectual life of the Catholic Church in the United States as well as for the way the Catholic Church in the United States perceives and responds "politically" to the huge social and cultural changes of these last fifty years. This book is also a response to the current refrains in the Catholic anti-conciliar pushback against Vatican II or in the more subtle "a-conciliar Catholicism"—as if Vatican II had never happened or got many things wrong (the anti-modernist narrative), or Vatican II is *passé* and has nothing to say to us today (the postmodernist approach).[2]

The title of this book has an emphasis on citizenship as part of the way many theologians live their vocation of doing theology. The idea of citizenship and the work of theology share sometimes the temptation to perceive themselves as *otium*, as leisure, while they

---

[1] For a powerful example of this American Catholic rendering of medieval Christianity, see Brad S. Gregory, *The Unintended Reformation: How a Religious Revolution Secularized Society* (Cambridge, MA: Harvard University Press, 2012). For the history of the influence of neo-scholastics in America beginning in the 1920s and 1930s, see Florian Michel, *La pensée catholique en Amérique du Nord. Réseaux intellectuels et échanges culturels entre l'Europe, le Canada et les États-Unis* (Paris: Desclée de Brouwer, 2010).

[2] For this recapturing of the idea that something actually happened at Vatican II and has something to tell us today, it is impossible to overestimate how much Catholics owe John W. O'Malley for his studies on the councils and for what his studies made possible during this last decade: John W. O'Malley and David G. Schultenover, eds., *Vatican II: Did Anything Happen?* (New York: Continuum, 2007) and especially John W. O'Malley, *What Happened at Vatican II* (Cambridge, MA: Belknap Press, 2008) and *Trent: What Happened at the Council* (Cambridge, MA: Belknap Press, 2013).

are in fact a *negotium*, an engagement with worldly affairs, a commitment requiring a certain amount of fidelity and of faith.

The second connotation of "citizenship" is the idea of citizenship as a theological concept related to the ecclesiology of the people of God, opposed to our fascination with leadership. It is another instance of the contamination of ecclesiology with language coming from corporate terminology. The corporatization of the university and of the church are not less dangerous than the politicization of them.

This book is a call to citizenship and a call for a culture of engagement and of encounter, in light of what the pontificate of Pope Francis says about the legacy of Vatican II and the role of the Catholic Church today. Recently Cathleen Kaveny synthesized, in the introduction of her book *A Culture of Engagement*, the history of the relations between Catholics and politics in the last few decades: from a culture of openness to a culture of identity, toward a culture of engagement and of encounter.[3] Pope Francis's pontificate questions the emphasis on identity and is a rediscovery of that openness, in the attempt to forge a new engagement and encounter, in a rejection of both Christian accommodationism and Christian separatism.

Francis opened a new phase in the reception of the Vatican II document most important for understanding his pontificate, *Gaudium et Spes*, which says: "This council exhorts Christians, as citizens of two cities, to strive to discharge their earthly duties conscientiously and in response to the Gospel spirit. They are mistaken who, knowing that we have here no abiding city but seek one which is to come, think that they may therefore shirk their earthly responsibilities. For they are forgetting that by the faith itself they are more obliged than ever to measure up to these duties, each according to their proper vocation" (GS 43).

Directly or indirectly, consciously or unconsciously, *Gaudium et Spes* is still *the debate* within Catholicism today, on the "signs of the times" of today, and on the method of doing theology. If we just look at the role of this document during the Bishops' Synods of 2014 and

---

[3] See Cathleen Kaveny, *A Culture of Engagement: Law, Religion, and Morality* (Washington, DC: Georgetown University Press, 2016), 3–11.

2015, in the texts and in the debates, it is clear that the role of the pastoral constitution is crucial for the future of the church.[4] For a church of the future there is no alternative to an honest but also full appropriation of *Gaudium et Spes*—not as a paradigmatic text, but as a model for the development of theological thinking. Francis has redefined the classic separation between church and society or church and world, but he has done that on the basis of a new appropriation of *Gaudium et Spes*.[5]

The world *huius temporis*—"of this time"—is very different from the world of 1962–1965. We live in a moment of crisis for our democratic systems, and the church is part of this crisis because there are historically very deep ties, despite all the appearances, between the long theological and institutional history of Catholicism and the much younger history of democracy. The crisis of democracy is also a theological crisis and as such it does not leave the church and theology untouched. This is especially true for the Catholic Church and Catholic theology.

The crisis of democracy and the crisis of the church are both rooted in the crisis of *representation*,[6] which in the German word *Repräsentation* carries three meanings: incarnation (*Inkarnation*), imagination (*Vorstellung*), and vicarial representation (*Stellvertretung*). There are many parallels between the crisis in our democratic systems and the crisis in the church—crisis of incarnation, of imagination, and of vicarial representation. Both are aspects of the crisis of postmodernism, which is to a large extent a crisis of representation

[4] See Antonio Spadaro, "Vocazione e missione della famiglia. Il XIV Sinodo dei Vescovi," *La Civiltà Cattolica* 3970 (November 28, 2015): 372–91.

[5] About this, see Christoph Theobald, "Mistica della fraternità. Lo stile nuovo della chiesa e della teologia nei documenti programmatici del pontificato," *Il Regno—attualità* 9 (2015): 581–88 (from the lecture delivered at the University of Vienna on October 15, 2015); in German: *"Mystik der Fraternité." Kirche und Theologie in neuem Stil*, in *Barmherzigkeit und zärtliche Liebe: Das theologische Programm von Papst Franziskus*, ed. Kurt Appel and Jakob Helmut Deibl (Freiburg i.Br.: Herder, 2016), 21–38.

[6] About this, see *Repraesentatio: Mapping a Keyword for Churches and Governance*, ed. Massimo Faggioli and Alberto Melloni (Berlin: LIT, 2006).

as the possibility of an organizing principle for modernity.[7] There is no superior part—not in the church, not in society—that can claim the privilege of representing the entire body politic or the entire church. Such representations simply do not exist anymore.[8]

Until a few years ago, the usual criticism was that the church could die for being too democratic; now, in this association between church and democracy, the church cannot look at democracy with a superiority complex, and vice versa. Religious secularization affects the church no less than political secularization affects our societies: emptying pews and emptying polling stations. Fr. Theodore Hesburgh called voting "the civic sacrament." There is a deep connection between the sacramentality of the church and the sacramentality of our staying together as citizens of a political community.

The crisis of our democracy calls Catholics to new responsibilities and this book is, in its own way, a call to citizenship. The way the Church will *represent* itself in the public square—with the liturgy, with its intellectual life, with its engagement for justice, with its works of mercy—will be a contribution to the earthly city that will say something also about its understanding of the City of God.

[7] About this, see Hasso Hofmann, *Repräsentation. Studien zur Wort und Begriffsgeschichte von der Antike bis ins 19. Jahrhundert* (Berlin: Duncker & Humblot, 1st ed. 1974, 4th ed. 2003).

[8] See Niklas Luhmann, *Gesellschaftsstruktur und Semantik*, vol. 3 (Frankfurt a.M.: Suhrkamp, 1989), and *Die Wissenschaft der Gesellschaft* (Frankfurt a.M.: Suhrkamp, 1992).

Bibliography

Alberigo, Giuseppe, ed. *History of Vatican II*. 5 vols. English version edited by Joseph A. Komonchak. Maryknoll, NY: Orbis Books, 1995–2006.

Brigham, Erin, ed. *The Church in the Modern World: Fifty Years after Gaudium et Spes*. Lanham, MD: Lexington Books, 2015.

Cavanaugh, William T. *Field Hospital: The Church's Engagement with a Wounded World*. Grand Rapids, MI: Eerdmans, 2016.

———. *Migrations of the Holy: God, State, and the Political Meaning of the Church*. Grand Rapids, MI: Eerdmans, 2011.

Congar, Yves. *Pour une Église servante et pauvre*. Paris: Cerf, 1963.

———. *Power and Poverty in the Church: The Renewal and Understanding of Service*. Mahwah, NJ: Paulist Press, 2016.

Congar, Yves, and Michel Peuchmaurd, eds. *L'Église dans le monde de ce temps*. 3 vols. Paris: Cerf, 1967.

Dianich, Severino. *Diritto e teologia. Ecclesiologia e canonistica per una riforma della Chiesa*. Bologna: EDB, 2015.

Eagleton, Terry. *Culture*. New Haven, CT: Yale University Press, 2016.

———. *The Illusions of Postmodernism*. Oxford: Blackwell, 1996.

———. *Reason, Faith, and Revolution: Reflections on the God Debate*. New Haven, CT: Yale University Press, 2009.

Faggioli, Massimo. *Pope Francis: Tradition in Transition*. Mahwah, NJ: Paulist Press, 2015.

———. *The Rising Laity: Ecclesial Movements since Vatican II*. Mahwah, NJ: Paulist Press, 2016.

———. *Sorting Out Catholicism: A Brief History of the New Ecclesial Movements*. Collegeville, MN: Liturgical Press, 2014.

Faggioli, Massimo, and Alberto Melloni, eds. *Repraesentatio: Mapping a Keyword for Churches and Governance*. Berlin: LIT, 2006.

Galli, Carlos Maria. *Dio vive in città. Verso una nuova pastorale urbana*. Preface by Andrea Riccardi. Vatican City: Libreria Editrice Vaticana, 2014.

Gaillardetz, Richard R., and Edward P. Hahnenberg, eds. *A Church with Open Doors: Catholic Ecclesiology for the Third Millennium.* Collegeville, MN: Liturgical Press, 2015.

Hartog, François. *Regimes of Historicity: Presentism and Experiences of Time.* Translated by Saskia Brown. New York: Columbia University Press, 2015; original French, 2002.

Hilberath, Bernd Jochen, and Peter Hünermann, eds. *Herders Theologischer Kommentar zum Zweiten Vatikanischen Konzil.* Vols. 1–5. Freiburg i.Br: Herder, 2004–2005.

Hofmann, Hasso. *Repräsentation. Studien zur Wort und Begriffsgeschichte von der Antike bis ins 19. Jahrhundert.* Berlin: Duncker & Humblot, 1974; 4th ed., 2003.

Hünermann, Peter, ed. *Das Zweite Vatikanische Konzil und die Zeichen der Zeit heute.* Freiburg i.Br.: Herder, 2006.

———. *Die Dokumente des Zweiten Vatikanischen Konzils. Zweisprachige Studienausgabe.* Freiburg i.Br.: Herder, 2012.

Huntington, Samuel P. *The Third Wave: Democratization in the Late Twentieth Century.* Norman: University of Oklahoma Press, 1991.

Kaiser, Wolfram. *Christian Democracy and the Origins of European Union.* Cambridge, UK: Cambridge University Press, 2011.

Kasper, Walter. *Mercy: The Essence of the Gospel and the Key to Christian Life.* Mahwah, NJ: Paulist Press, 2014.

———. *Pope Francis' Revolution of Tenderness and Love.* Translated by William Madges. Mahwah, NJ: Paulist Press, 2015.

Kaufmann, Franz-Xaver. *Kirche in der ambivalenten Moderne.* Freiburg i.Br.: Herder, 2012.

Kaveny, Cathleen. *A Culture of Engagement: Law, Religion, and Morality.* Washington, DC: Georgetown University Press, 2016.

Konieczny, Mary Ellen, Charles C. Camosy, and Tricia C. Bruce, eds. *Polarization in the US Catholic Church: Naming the Wounds, Beginning to Heal.* Collegeville, MN: Liturgical Press, 2016.

McEvoy, James Gerard. *Leaving Christendom for Good: Church-World Dialogue in a Secular Age.* Lanham, MD: Lexington Books, 2014.

Morra, Stella. *Dio non si stanca. La misericordia come forma ecclesiale.* Bologna: EDB, 2015.

Nacke, Stefan. *Die Kirche der Weltgesellschaft. Das II. Vatikanische Konzil und die Globalisierung des Katholizismus.* Wiesbaden: VS Verlag, 2010.

Neri, Marcello. *Giustizia come misericordia. Europa, cristianesimo e spiritualità dehoniana.* Bologna: EDB, 2016.

Oakley, Francis. *The Conciliarist Tradition: Constitutionalism in the Catholic Church 1300–1870*. New York: Oxford University Press, 2003.

O'Malley, John W. *What Happened at Vatican II*. Cambridge, MA: Belknap Press, 2008.

———. *Trent: What Happened at the Council*. Cambridge, MA: Belknap Press, 2013.

Ormerod, Neil. *Re-Visioning the Church: An Experiment in Systematic-Historical Ecclesiology*. Minneapolis: Fortress, 2014.

Perreau-Saussine, Emile. *Catholicism and Democracy: An Essay in the History of Political Thought*. Princeton, NJ: Princeton University Press, 2012.

Prodi, Paolo. *Il tramonto della rivoluzione*. Bologna: Il Mulino, 2015.

———. *Università dentro e fuori*. Bologna: Il Mulino, 2013.

Przywara, Erich. *L'idea d'Europa. La "crisi" di ogni politica "cristiana."* Edited by Fabrizio Mandreoli and José Luis Narvaja. Torino: Il pozzo di Giacobbe, 2013.

Rahner, Karl. *Theological Investigations*. Vol. 20: *Concern for the Church*. Translated by Edward Quinn. New York: Crossroad, 1981.

Sander, Hans-Joachim. "Aggiornamento—Kennzeichen nur des Konzils? Der spatial turn des Glaubens durch das Zweite Vatikanische Konzil." *Theologie und Glaube* 102 (2012): 510–25.

———. "Theologischer Kommentar zur Pastoralkonstitution über die Kirche in der Welt von heute." In *Herders Theologischer Kommentar zum Zweiten Vatikanischen Konzil*, edited by Bernd Jochen Hilberath and Peter Hünermann. Vol. 5, 581–886. Freiburg i.Br.: Herder, 2005.

———. "Vom religionsgemeinschaftlichen Urbi et Orbi zu pastoralgemeinschaftlichen Heterotopien. Eine Topologie Gottes in den Zeichen der Zeit." In *Zweites Vatikanisches Konzil: Programmatik—Rezeption—Vision*, edited by Christoph Böttigheimer, 157–79. Freiburg i.Br.: Herder, 2014.

Scatena, Silvia. *La fatica della libertà. L'elaborazione della dichiarazione "Dignitatis humanae" sulla libertà religiosa del Vaticano II*. Bologna: Il Mulino, 2003.

Schickendantz, Carlos. "Una eclipse con dos focos: hacia un nuevo método teológico a partir de *Gaudium et Spes*." *Teología* 50, no. 110 (April 2013): 85–109.

———. "¿Una transformación metodológica inadvertida? La novedad introducida por *Gaudium et Spes* en los escritos de Joseph Ratzinger." *Teología y Vida* 57, no. 1 (2016): 9–37.

Schlabach, Gerald W. "The Virtue of Staying Put: What the 'Benedict Option' Forgets about Benedictines." *Commonweal* (October 7, 2016): 11–13.

Schloesser, Stephen R. "'Dancing on the Edge of the Volcano': Biopolitics and What Happened after Vatican II." In *From Vatican II to Pope Francis: Charting a Catholic Future*, edited by Paul Crowley, 3–26. Maryknoll, NY: Orbis Books, 2014.

Schneiders, Sandra. *Buying the Field: Catholic Religious Life in Mission to the World*. Religious Life in a New Millennium 3. Mahwah, NJ: Paulist Press, 2013.

Simmonds, Gemma, ed. *A Future Built on Faith: Religious Life and the Legacy of Vatican II*. Dublin: Columba, 2014.

Steinfels, Peter. *A People Adrift: The Crisis of the Roman Catholic Church in America*. New York: Simon & Schuster, 2003.

Taylor, Charles. *A Secular Age*. Cambridge, MA: Belknap Press, 2007.

Theobald, Christoph. *Le Concile Vatican II. Quel avenir?* Paris: Cerf, 2015.

———. *La réception du concile Vatican II*. Vol. 1, *Accéder à la source*. Paris: Cerf, 2009.

Turbanti, Giovanni. *Un concilio per il mondo moderno. La redazione della costituzione pastorale "Gaudium et spes" del Vaticano II*. Bologna: Il Mulino, 2000.

Vorgrimler, Herbert, ed. *Commentary on the Documents of Vatican II*. 5 vols. New York: Herder and Herder, 1969.

Zamagni, Gianmaria. *Fine dell'era costantiniana. Retrospettiva genealogica di un concetto critico*. Bologna: Il Mulino, 2012 (*Das "Ende des konstantinischen Zeitalters" und die Modelle aus der Geschichte für eine "Neue Christenheit". Eine religionsgeschichtliche Untersuchung*. Freiburg i.Br.: Herder, 2016).

Index